VISUAL QUICKSTART GUIDE

.MAC WITH IWEB

SECOND EDITION

David Reynolds

 Peachpit Press

Visual QuickStart Guide
.Mac with iWeb, Second Edition
David Reynolds

Peachpit Press

1249 Eighth Street
Berkeley, CA 94710
510/524-2178
800/283-9444
510/524-2221 (fax)

Find us on the World Wide Web at: www.peachpit.com
To report errors, please send a note to errata@peachpit.com

Peachpit Press is a division of Pearson Education

Editor: Jim Akin
Production editor: Becky Winter
Copy editor: Eliss Rabellino
Compositor: Chris Gillespie, Happenstance Type-O-Rama
Indexer: James Minkin
Cover design: Peachpit Press

Notice of Rights

Notice of Rights

Trademarks

ISBN 0-321-44228-8

9 8 7 6 5 4

Printed and bound in the United States of America

Dedication

This book is dedicated to my father, who made me a far better man than I would have been had I not known him.

Acknowledgments

I'd like to thank the following people, without whom... well, I shudder to think about it.

My wife Susan and sons Ben and Jake, for their tolerance and reminders about what really matters in life.

My good friend and excellent editor Nikki McDonald, who is a joy to work with—even if she does push me to be a better writer.

I'd also like to thank Jim Akin, who not only shepherded this book through its latest revision, he also helped me with the heavy lifting—and has a great sense of humor to boot.

The good folks at Peachpit Press—Cliff Colby, Elissa Rabellino, Sean McDonald, Simmy Cover, Sara Jane Todd, Jackie Hill, Kim Becker, Becky Winter, Damon Hampson and everyone else—who gave me this opportunity and who worked so hard to make a quality book.

TABLE OF CONTENTS

TABLE OF CONTENTS

TABLE OF CONTENTS

GETTING STARTED

Back at the turn of the millennium, Apple came out with a suite of Internet tools called iTools, which consisted of a *mac.com* e-mail address as well as KidSafe (a filter for child-friendly Web sites), HomePage (an easy-to-use tool for building Web sites), and iDisk (20 MB of online storage that was accessible using just about any Internet connection). Apple's Internet strategy basically boiled down to a nifty set of Mac-only tools meant to make Mac users' online lives a little easier.

Fast-forward half a dozen years. The tools are no longer free and the name has changed—iTools now goes by .Mac (pronounced "dot mac")—but the goal remains the same: make Mac users' online lives easier. With a *mac.com* e-mail address, iDisk, and HomePage still at its core, .Mac now also includes tight integration with Mac OS X, as well as a host of other features, all for just $99 a year. Sounds expensive until you look at it this way: It amounts to just 27 cents a day. If you're like me, you can find that under your couch cushions, along with a few stale snacks.

In this chapter, I'll show you how to create your .Mac account, set your .Mac preferences, manage your .Mac account, and set up your iDisk.

About .Mac

.Mac isn't just a single application or Web site. It's a suite of Internet services that's meant to help Mac users get more from their Macs. I'll quickly walk through each of the .Mac services now before going into greater detail on how to use each one later in the book.

◆ **.Mac Mail.** At the center of your .Mac membership is a full e-mail account ending in *@mac.com*. You can use this e-mail account to send and receive e-mail on any computer that has a POP or IMAP client available, and that's pretty much every one out there. In addition, .Mac Mail is Web based, so you can send and receive e-mail from any Web browser.

◆ **iDisk.** All .Mac accounts come with 1 GB of online storage that you can use to keep mail and files on your iDisk. Support for iDisk is built into Mac OS X, and using it is a lot like using any other network server—or even a hard drive, for that matter. iDisk serves as the backbone for publishing Web pages and synchronizing information between Macs.

◆ **iLife '06 Integration.** With iWeb and iPhoto, members of the iLife suite of applications, you can easily publish Web pages and sites to your .Mac account, as well as create shareable photo albums called Photocasts. And with GarageBand, you can create your own high-quality enhanced podcasts, complete with images, and share them through .Mac.

◆ **HomePage.** Your .Mac membership includes access to HomePage, handy Web-based software that allows you to quickly build Web pages that serve as photo albums, movie theaters, and file-download pages.

HomePage uses files that you upload to your iDisk. HomePage is also integrated with iPhoto, making it incredibly easy to share your pictures.

◆ **Groups.** Use your .Mac account to organize your soccer team, your grade-school classroom, or your online-gaming guild. A .Mac Group gives members a group e-mail, a message board, a calendar, and iDisk space—just for Group members.

◆ **Backup.** Each .Mac membership comes with Backup, a free utility designed to automate data backups to your .Mac account as well as to CDs, DVDs, and external hard drives. Making sure your important files get backed up doesn't sound very sexy, but when you're facing a corrupt hard drive and you don't have a backup, a simple and free backup utility starts looking pretty good.

◆ **Address Book.** Your .Mac account lets you synchronize your Address Book data so that it's available to you anywhere you have access to a Web browser. And with Mac OS X v10.4 Tiger, you can share your Address Book with others.

◆ **iCards.** With a .Mac account, you can create and send e-mail greeting cards, drawn from Apple's professionally designed assortment or chosen from your own custom creations.

◆ **.Mac Sync.** With Mac OS X v10.4, you can synchronize important information, such as Keychain passwords, Mail's Smart Mailboxes, and Safari bookmarks, to your .Mac account—which lets you keep that information in sync with another Mac and provides you with a backup copy. Even those running Mac OS X v10.3 Panther can use iSync with .Mac to keep their information synchronized across Macs.

ABOUT .MAC

Hardware and Software Requirements

You don't need much to run .Mac—its requirements are pretty minimal. To take advantage of .Mac and all of its features, you'll need a Macintosh running Mac OS X 10.3.9 or later, 128 MB of RAM, and an up-to-date browser such as Safari or Firefox. The iDisk Utility for Windows requires—you guessed it—a PC running Windows XP.

✔ Tip

■ You can find a full rundown of all .Mac system requirements at www.mac.com/1/systemrequirements.html.

.Mac Family Pack

.Mac provides a great way to give every member of your family his or her own not-so-little corner of your .Mac account. For $179.95 a year, you get five accounts: one master account and four subaccounts, each with a unique e-mail address, storage space, Web pages, and synchronization. The master account gets a full 1 GB of storage space (split between e-mail and iDisk), and each subaccount gets 250 MB of storage space (split between e-mail and storage).

Subscribing to the .Mac Newsletter

Although it's a good idea to be careful with your e-mail address—after all, one slip-up and you'll be getting more spam than you do now—subscribing to the .Mac Newsletter is a pretty good idea.

This newsletter contains special information and offers for .Mac members that can help you take full advantage of your .Mac account. And don't worry about being bombarded by too much e-mail—the frequency of these communiqués wouldn't bury anyone.

Configuring Mac OS X

After you've bought and paid for your .Mac account, you can go to www.mac.com, log in, and begin using some features—such as Mail—right away. However, to get the most out of your .Mac account, you'll want to configure your Mac's operating system to work with it by setting up your .Mac preferences. After all, one of the chief benefits of having a .Mac account is its tight integration with Mac OS X. If you entered your .Mac account information when installing Mac OS X, your operating system is already configured to work with your .Mac account. If, however, you ever need to change your .Mac login information (say, you change your .Mac account), you'll need to follow a similar procedure.

To set up Mac OS X to work with a .Mac account:

1. From the Apple menu, choose System Preferences (**Figure 1.1**).

   The System Preferences window opens.

2. *Do one of the following*:

   ▲ In the Internet & Network section, click the .Mac icon to select it (**Figure 1.2**).

   ▲ From the View menu, choose .Mac. The .Mac pane opens.

3. Click the Account tab to select it, if it is not already selected.

4. In the .Mac Member Name field, enter your .Mac member name.

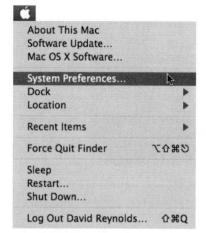

Figure 1.1 To set up Mac OS X to access your .Mac account, you'll need to first open System Preferences by choosing System Preferences from the Apple menu.

Figure 1.2 The .Mac preferences are nestled in the Internet & Network section of the System Preferences window. Click the .Mac globe icon, and the .Mac preference pane will load.

CONFIGURING MAC OS X

Figure 1.3 The Account tab of the .Mac preference pane asks for your .Mac member name and password, and it reminds you of how long you have until your account expires. This page offers more options in Mac OS X v10.4 than it did in earlier versions, including the new Sync area, in which you can choose what information gets synchronized, and the Advanced area, which shows which computers are registered to be synchronized.

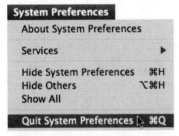

Figure 1.4 When you quit System Preferences, any changes you make to the .Mac pane are saved automatically.

5. In the Password field, enter your password (**Figure 1.3**).

6. From the System Preferences menu, choose Quit System Preferences (Command-Q) (**Figure 1.4**).

Mac OS X is now set up to access your .Mac account.

✔ Tips

■ You can choose whatever you like for your password, as long as it's 6 to 14 characters long. Make sure it's something you can remember but isn't easy to guess.

■ If you don't yet have a .Mac account, click the Learn More button in the lower right portion of the .Mac preference pane. This takes you to the .Mac homepage, where you can become a .Mac member by purchasing an annual .Mac subscription.

CONFIGURING MAC OS X

Changing Account Settings

Your .Mac account has a wide range of settings that you can only change online. If you want to make changes to your personal information, credit card information, password, or e-mail settings—or if you want to purchase additional iDisk space—you need to first log in to your .Mac account using a Web browser.

To log in to your .Mac account settings:

1. Type www.mac.com in your Web browser. The .Mac Web page opens (**Figure 1.5**).

2. In the upper left corner of the .Mac page, click Account to select it (**Figure 1.6**). Your .Mac login page opens.

Figure 1.5 Welcome to .Mac! When you first load the .Mac homepage in a Web browser, you'll be greeted by a page that looks like this (although it may be different, since Web pages can change on a dime).

Figure 1.6 In the upper left corner of the .Mac homepage you'll see the Account link. Click it to load the login page of your .Mac account.

About the Other Settings

The Account Settings page also covers settings that relate to your .Mac e-mail account and your iDisk. These settings let you do the following:

◆ Change e-mail account settings. (For more information, see Chapter 2, "Sending Mail.")

◆ Manage and buy more e-mail accounts. (For more information, see Chapter 2, "Sending Mail.")

◆ Check iDisk usage via a Web browser. (For more information, see Chapter 3, "Using iDisk.")

◆ Buy more online storage. (For more information, see Chapter 3, "Using iDisk.")

Figure 1.7 To log in to .Mac, enter your .Mac member name and password, and then click the Login button.

3. In the Member name field, type your .Mac e-mail address. You can also use your member name—it's the portion of your .Mac e-mail address that precedes the @ symbol. (**Figure 1.7**).

4. In the Password field, type your password.

5. Click the Login button.

Your .Mac Account Settings page opens, and you can now make changes to your account (**Figure 1.8**).

✔ Tip

- If you've forgotten your .Mac password, you can click the "Forgot your password?" link on the login page to retrieve it.

Figure 1.8 This is your main .Mac Account Settings page. Here you can manage your e-mail accounts, buy more storage, and change your personal information, credit card information, and a plethora of other settings.

CHANGING ACCOUNT SETTINGS

To change your personal information:

1. Log in to your .Mac account settings as described in "To log in to your .Mac account settings ".

   The Account Settings page opens.

2. On the Account Settings page, click the Personal Info button as shown in Figure 1.8.

   Your Personal Info page opens (**Figure 1.9**).

3. On the Personal Info page, *do any of the following:*

   ▲ In the First Name field, change your first name.

   ▲ In the Last Name field, change your last name.

   ▲ In the Alternate Email Address field, change or edit your alternate e-mail address (where you can be contacted regarding .Mac, in case your .Mac address isn't available for some reason).

   ▲ In the Preferred Language pop-up menu, select your preferred language in which to view .Mac (currently the options are English, French, German, and Japanese).

   ▲ In the News and Info section, check the box to change your opt-in e-mail setting (when checked, this tells Apple that you don't mind being sent the .Mac Newsletter and other .Mac communications).

4. Click the Submit button.

   Apple applies the changes you made to your .Mac account's personal information settings.

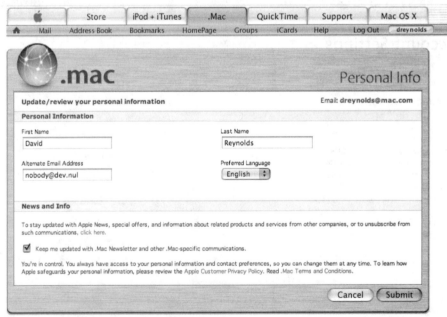

Figure 1.9 Your .Mac Personal Info page lets you change your member name, assign an alternate e-mail address, set your preferred language, and request a subscription to the .Mac Newsletter. The newsletter is well worth subscribing to, and it's free to .Mac members.

Figure 1.10 Your .Mac Credit Card Info page lets you adjust settings that include your credit card type and number, your name and billing address, and auto-renewal of your account.

Changing credit card information

.Mac is built around an annual subscription, and therefore it keeps your credit card information on file (just in case you want to sign up for the optional automatic renewal). Of course, as soon as you get that new card with 0 percent interest on all balance transfers and new purchases, you'll probably want to change the credit card information stored in your .Mac account.

To change your credit card information:

1. Log in to your .Mac account settings as described in "To log in to your .Mac account settings".

   The Account Settings page opens.

2. On the Account Settings page, click the Credit Card Info button, as shown in Figure 1.8.

   The Credit Card Info page opens (**Figure 1.10**).

3. On the Credit Card Info page, *do any of the following*:
   ▲ Change your credit card number and billing information.
   ▲ Check the Auto-Renew box to set your .Mac membership to automatically renew.
   ▲ If the Auto-Renew check box is already selected and you don't want your .Mac membership to automatically renew, click the check box to deselect it.

4. Click Submit.

   Apple applies the changes you made to your .Mac account's credit card settings.

✔ Tip

■ If you do select the Auto-Renew check box on the Credit Card Info settings page, you'll get an e-mail about 30 days before your account is set to automatically renew, notifying you of the impending action.

Changing password settings

When logged in to your .Mac account settings, you can also change your .Mac password and your .Mac password verification, including your birthday, password question, and password answer.

To change your password settings:

1. Log in to your .Mac account settings as described in "To log in to your .Mac account settings ".

   The Account Settings page opens.

2. On the Account Settings page, click the Password Settings button, as shown in Figure 1.8.

   Your Password Settings page opens (**Figure 1.11**).

3. On the Password Settings page, *do any of the following:*
   - ▲ In the Password fields, type a new password and confirm it.
   - ▲ From the Date of Birth pop-up menus, change your birth date.
   - ▲ In the Password Question field, type a new password question.
   - ▲ In the Password Answer field, type a new answer to your password question.

4. Click Submit.

   Apple applies the changes you made to your .Mac account's password settings.

Figure 1.11. Your .Mac Password Settings page lets you change your password (although you can't view it—all you see is bullets). You can also use it to set password-verification information—namely, your birthday and a password question and answer.

In Case You Don't Have a .Mac Account

If you've bought this book, we're assuming that you've taken the plunge and signed up for a .Mac account. Congratulations! It'll change your life.

If you're browsing this book, however, and you're contemplating a purchase, you might not yet have a .Mac account. Getting one is easy; all you need is a credit card, an Internet connection, and a Web browser.

To sign up as a .Mac member, visit www.mac.com and click the Join Now button on the front page. You'll be asked to provide a credit card number, preferred member name, billing address, password, and the like. Signing up is painless and takes only a few minutes. So what are you waiting for? And if you're a box-and-disc kind of person, you can purchase .Mac at the Apple Store or from some authorized resellers.

SENDING MAIL

One of the biggest benefits of having a .Mac account is that you get an e-mail address that moves with you, even if you switch ISPs— no more sending out those "my e-mail address has changed" messages, asking everyone to update their address books (which no one does). Plus, if you're like me, you get the cachet of an e-mail address that associates your messages with a computer you love.

Your .Mac e-mail account uses your .Mac login name with *@mac.com* as your e-mail address. You can use your .Mac e-mail account with just about any e-mail client program out there—provided it can use POP3 or IMAP, and that covers almost any you care to name. In this chapter, I'll show you how to set up your e-mail client to work with your .Mac e-mail account. You'll also learn how to use .Mac Mail on the Web, which allows you to work with your e-mail using just about any Web browser.

Setting Up Apple Mail

Apple has integrated .Mac e-mail into its own e-mail client, Mail. Since Apple owns both Mail and .Mac, you can expect them to work very well together. (Don't be fooled, though—.Mac plays well with other e-mail clients, too.)

There are three scenarios for setting up Mail to use your .Mac e-mail account:

◆ You haven't opened Mail but have entered your .Mac subscription information in System Preferences.

◆ You haven't opened Mail and haven't entered your .Mac subscription information in System Preferences.

◆ You have already opened Mail (whether or not you've entered your .Mac subscription information in System Preferences).

✔ Tip

■ Your .Mac e-mail account isn't the only wrench in the toolbox. .Mac also lets you send classy and custom e-mail greeting cards (called iCards), and it enables you to connect to other .Mac and AOL Instant Messenger users via iChat.

POP vs. IMAP

Most e-mail accounts come in two flavors: the old-school, client-based POP (or POP3), and the newer, server-based IMAP. What's the difference? POP (short for Post Office Protocol) accounts download all of your mail to your computer when you connect, whereas IMAP (short for Internet Message Access Protocol) accounts keep the mail on the server and let you read it from your computer—making it easy to read your e-mail from anywhere but requiring you to stay connected to the Internet whenever you work with your e-mail—even for reading or moving messages. Your .Mac e-mail account can act as either a POP or IMAP account, depending on which you prefer. So, which should you choose?

One drawback of an IMAP account is that your stored mail counts toward your .Mac storage protocol. Another is that you must be connected to the Internet to organize or sort your mail—even mail you've already read.

You should use IMAP if:

◆ You use several computers to access your mail.

◆ You have an always-on connection that you can use while you work with your mail.

You should use a POP account if:

◆ You use only one computer to access your e-mail.

◆ You like the idea of keeping your mail on your computer and not on a server.

◆ You work with your mail when you're not connected to the Internet.

Figure 2.1 When you first launch Mail, it asks if you want to import mailboxes from another e-mail client, which is great if you've been using a different client and want to take the leap to Mail. Click Yes to import mailboxes; click No to skip this step and move on.

Figure 2.2 Next, Mail asks if you'd like to see what's new in this version. Click Yes to take a tour; click No to skip this step and move on.

If you haven't opened Mail but have entered your .Mac subscription information

This is typically the case if you've just installed a fresh copy of Mac OS X and entered your .Mac information in the setup assistant but you haven't yet fired up Mail. Typically, folks who already have a .Mac account fall into this category.

If you're using Mac OS X v10.4 Tiger and you've entered your .Mac information in System Preferences, Mac OS X automatically creates an account for you in Mail. All you have to do is open the Mail application.

To set up Mail with your .Mac e-mail address (Mac OS X 10.3 or earlier):

1. In the Applications folder, double-click the Mail icon to open Mail.

   The Mail application opens, and you're asked if you want to import mailboxes from another client (**Figure 2.1**).

2. Click No.

   Mail then notes that this version is greatly enhanced and asks if you'd like to take a tour (**Figure 2.2**).

3. Click No.

   Mac OS X automatically configures Mail to work with your .Mac e-mail address. You are ready to use Mail to send and receive mail with your .Mac account.

SETTING UP APPLE MAIL

If you haven't opened Mail and haven't entered your .Mac subscription information

This usually happens if you set up your Mac before you had a .Mac subscription (and thus didn't enter anything in the setup assistant) and you haven't been using Mail as your e-mail client. We'll show you how to do this using Mac OS X v10.3 Jaguar as well as with Mac OS X v10.4.

To set up Mail to work with your .Mac e-mail address (Mac OS X v10.4):

1. In the Applications folder, double-click the Mail icon to open Mail.

   The Mail setup assistant opens (**Figure 2.3**).

2. Click Continue.

   The General Information pane opens (**Figure 2.4**).

3. From the Account Type pop-up menu, choose .Mac.

4. In the Account Description field, give the account a description.

5. In the Full Name field, type your name.

Figure 2.3 This is the first pane in the Mac OS X 10.4 Mail setup assistant. Click Continue to move to the next step.

Figure 2.4 The General Information pane asks you to choose your account type, provide an account description and your full name, and provide your e-mail user name and password. Click Continue to move to the next step after you've filled in all the fields.

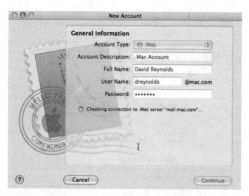

Figure 2.5 After you've clicked Continue, Mail checks the information you've entered to ensure that all of the connections are good.

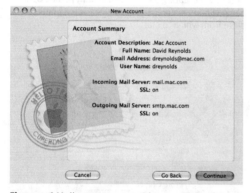

Figure 2.6 Mail presents you with a summary of your new Mail account settings.

Figure 2.7 Finally, when your account is created, you can choose to import mail, create another account, or click the Done button and go on about your business.

6. In the User Name field, type your .Mac member name.

7. In the Password field, type your .Mac password.

8. Click Continue.

Mail checks your connection information to make sure you can connect (**Figure 2.5**). After this check is complete, a summary pane opens (**Figure 2.6**).

9. Click Continue.

The Conclusion pane opens, offering you the choice of importing mailboxes or creating another account (**Figure 2.7**).

10. Click Done to finish.

You're ready to use Mac OS X v10.4 Mail to send and receive e-mail with your .Mac e-mail address.

To set up Mail to work with your .Mac e-mail address (Mac OS X v10.3 or earlier):

1. In the Applications folder, double-click the Mail icon to open Mail.

   The Mail application opens, and you're asked to set up an account (**Figure 2.8**).

2. In the Full Name field, type your name.

3. In the Email Address field, type your .Mac e-mail address, which is your .Mac member name plus *@mac.com*.

4. In the Incoming Mail Server field, type `mail.mac.com`.

5. From the Account Type pop-up menu, choose POP or IMAP (see the sidebar "POP vs. IMAP").

6. In the User Name field, type your .Mac login.

7. In the Password field, type your .Mac password.

8. In the Outgoing Mail Server (SMTP) field, type `smtp.mac.com`.

9. Click OK (**Figure 2.9**). You're asked if you want to import mail from another client (**Figure 2.10**).

Figure 2.8 Creating a new Mail account in Mac OS X v10.3 is fairly simple, and Mail gives you a blank slate from which to start.

Figure 2.9 After you've filled in the pertinent information, you can click OK to create your account.

Figure 2.10 Again, Mail asks if you care to bring e-mail messages over from another e-mail program. You'd click Yes to import mail messages, but for now click No to skip this step.

Welcome

This version of Mail is greatly enhanced with new features, improvements, and optimizations. For details, choose Mail Help from the Help menu.

Would you like to see what's new?

No Yes

Figure 2.11 Again, Mail asks if you'd like to see what's new in this version. Click Yes to take a tour; click No to skip this step and move on.

10. Click No.

    You're asked if you want to find out about the new features in Mail (**Figure 2.11**).

11. You can click Yes another time for a pleasant tour, but for now click No.

    You're ready to use Mail to send and receive e-mail with your .Mac e-mail address.

Setting Up E-mail Software Other Than Apple Mail

Setting up another e-mail client to work with your .Mac e-mail account is similar to setting up Mail—mostly, you need to enter a few bits of information in a window much like the one used for Mail. This information consists of your e-mail address, incoming-mail-server address, outgoing-mail-server address, user name and password, and any authentication that your servers need.

You can use your .Mac account with any POP or IMAP e-mail client, whether on Windows, the Mac OS, or Linux (or pretty much any other operating system that has a POP or IMAP client available). The same method should apply to any e-mail client.

To set up another e-mail client to use your .Mac e-mail account:

1. Open the e-mail client.

2. Create a new account in your e-mail client. Typically, you'll look under a menu named Preferences, Tools, or Accounts (you may need to consult the e-mail client's help system).

3. Choose IMAP or POP for the account type.

4. In the field for the incoming e-mail server, enter mail.mac.com.

5. In the account ID field, enter your .Mac member ID.

6. In the password field, enter your .Mac password.

7. In the outgoing-mail-server field, enter smtp.mac.com.

8. In the SMTP-authentication fields, enter your .Mac member name and password.

9. Check to ensure that SMTP authentication is turned on for this account.

The account should be ready to send and receive e-mail using your .Mac e-mail account.

If you've already opened Mail

If you've opened Mail but haven't entered your .Mac information, you need to manually configure your account. This simply means that you need to provide more information when setting up your account.

To set up Mail to work with your .Mac e-mail address (Mac OS X 10.4):

1. In the Applications folder, double-click the Mail icon to open Mail.

   The Mail application opens.

2. From the Mail menu, choose Preferences (**Figure 2.12**).

   Mail's Preferences window opens with the Account Information tab selected and the Accounts pane opens. (**Figure 2.13**).

3. In the lower left corner of the window, click the plus (+) button.

   Mail's setup assistant opens to the General Information pane, as shown in Figure 2.4.

4. From the Account Type pop-up menu, choose .Mac.

5. In the Account Description field, give the account a description.

6. In the Full Name field, type your name.

7. In the User Name field, type your .Mac member name.

Figure 2.12 To access Mail's preferences, choose Preferences from the Mail menu or press Command-, (comma).

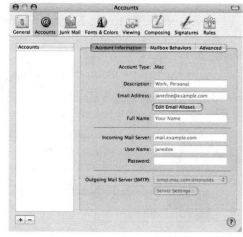

Figure 2.13 Using Mail's Accounts preferences, you can create and manage e-mail accounts in Mail. Here, no e-mail accounts exist yet.

Figure 2.14 Once you've entered your .Mac account information, the Account Summary sheet shows you how the account has been set up.

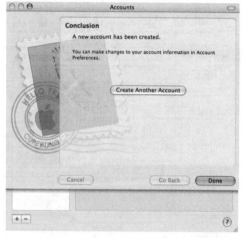

Figure 2.15 After your account has been created, Mail gives you the option of creating another account or simply clicking Done on the lower-right portion of the page and moving on with your life.

8. In the Password field, type your .Mac password.

9. Click Continue.

   Mail checks your connection information to make sure you can connect. After this check is complete, the Account Summary sheet slides down over the window (**Figure 2.14**).

10. Click Continue.

    The Conclusion sheet opens, offering you the chance to create another account (**Figure 2.15**).

11. Click Done.

    You're ready to use Mac OS X v10.4 Mail to send and receive e-mail with your .Mac e-mail address.

SETTING UP APPLE MAIL

To set up Mail to work with your .Mac e-mail address (Mac OS X v10.3):

1. In the Applications folder, double-click the Mail icon to open Mail.

   The Mail application opens.

2. From the Mail menu, choose Preferences, as shown in Figure 2.12.

   Mail's Preferences window opens.

3. If it's not already selected, click the Accounts button.

   The Accounts pane opens (**Figure 2.16**).

4. In the lower left corner of the window, click the plus (+) button.

   A new Mail account is created, and the Account Information tab is automatically selected (**Figure 2.17**).

Figure 2.16 Mail's Accounts preferences let you create and manage e-mail accounts in Mail. Here, no e-mail accounts exist yet.

Figure 2.17 After you click the plus (+) button, the name of a new account appears in the column on the left, and the fields on the right are ready to fill in.

Figure 2.18 Mail supports these four types of e-mail accounts: .Mac, POP, IMAP, and Exchange. For our purposes, select .Mac (and note that .Mac e-mail will also work with POP and IMAP).

Figure 2.19 Once you've finished entering the account information, close this window; Mail will now be able to send and receive e-mail using your .Mac account. This is how the window looks when everything is filled in. Note that what used to read New Account on the left has now changed to the account name you typed in the Description field.

5. From the Account Type pop-up menu, choose .Mac (**Figure 2.18**).

6. In the Description field, type a short description of your account (such as your name or your business name—typically a few words).

7. In the Full Name field, type your name.

8. In the User Name field, type your .Mac member name.

9. In the Password field, type your .Mac password.

Mail fills in the Email Address, Incoming Mail Server, and Outgoing Mail Server fields for you.

10. Click the red close button in the upper left corner to close the window (**Figure 2.19**).

You're ready to use Mail to send and receive e-mail with your .Mac e-mail address. The account is added to any other e-mail accounts you've already set up in Mail.

Using Webmail

Using an e-mail client (such as Apple's Mail or Microsoft's Entourage) isn't the only way to access your .Mac e-mail account. Your .Mac account also gives you Webmail, so you can send and receive e-mail, organize your e-mail, and even use the addresses stored in Mac OS X's Address Book from anywhere you have a Web browser and access to the Internet.

To open .Mac Webmail:

1. Open your Web browser and go to http://Webmail.mac.com.

   The .Mac login page opens.

2. In the Member name field, type your .Mac member name.

3. In the Password field, type your .Mac password (**Figure 2.20**).

4. Click Login.

   The Web browser loads your .Mac e-mail Inbox page (**Figure 2.21**). This Web page looks and behaves a lot like an e-mail client, and if you've ever used Web-based mail for other e-mail accounts, you'll probably feel right at home. The Inbox page features a toolbar across the top, a message count and search field, a list of messages, and a message count at the bottom—everything you need to work with your e-mail.

Figure 2.20 You'll be seeing a lot of this page. This is the .Mac login page, and you'll use it to enter your .Mac member name and password to access the members' area of the .Mac Web site.

Figure 2.21 The .Mac Webmail Inbox page looks and behaves a lot like an application-based e-mail program does. Icons across the top act like buttons in a program, causing actions to happen. E-mail messages are listed below the buttons.

✔ Tips

- .Mac Webmail displays the contents of your e-mail inbox by default. To view your other e-mail folders, select them from the "Go To:" popup in the Webmail toolbar, or list all folders by choosing Show All Folders from the popup. (Note that some folders exist only when there are messages stored inside them; you won't have a Sent Mail folder until you've sent a message, for instance.)

- To sort listed messages, click the column header above what you want to sort by (such as date, message size, or subject).

- You can also visit www.mac.com, log in to your .Mac account, and then click the Mail button. This also will take you to the Web interface for your .Mac e-mail account.

- If you're using IMAP with your .Mac account, you can manage your mail by logging in to your .Mac account through a Web browser. From there, you can move and delete mail, for example, and create and delete folders. These changes will show up in your IMAP e-mail client the next time you synchronize your mail.

To read a message:

◆ Click the subject line of the message you want to read (**Figure 2.22**).

or

◆ Click the name of the person who sent the message.

The message loads in your browser's Mail window.

✔ Tip

■ When reading a message, you can move to the previous message or next message by using your arrow keys, or you can move back to the list of messages by clicking the Mail button.

To delete a message:

1. Click the subject line or the name of the person who sent the message you want to delete.

The message loads in your Mail window.

2. Click the Delete button (**Figure 2.23**).

The message is moved to the Deleted Messages folder, and the next message is displayed.

✔ Tip

■ You can also delete one or more messages directly from the .Mac e-mail Inbox page, by clicking the checkboxes to the left of the name(s) of the senders(s) whose message(s) you want to delete, then checking the circle-with-a-slash Delete button in Webmail toolbar.

Figure 2.22 Click the subject line of a message to open and read it. Because this is a Web page and not an e-mail program, the message will not be highlighted when it is clicked—but your pointer will change to indicate that it is over something you can click.

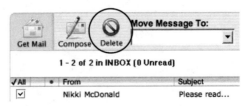

Figure 2.23 Click the Delete button to delete the message you're reading.

Figure 2.24 Click the Reply button to move to .Mac's reply-composition page, where you can pen a reply to a message you've received.

Figure 2.25 When you compose a reply to a message, you'll see a few key things—the recipient's e-mail address, the subject line, and your reply text.

Figure 2.26 Click the Send button to send your message.

To reply to a message:

1. Click the subject line of the message to which you want to reply.

   The message loads in the Inbox window.

2. Click the Reply button (**Figure 2.24**).

   This takes you to the message-composition page, where you can write your reply in the text box (**Figure 2.25**).

3. Type your reply, and then click the Send button (**Figure 2.26**).

   Your reply is sent to the person who sent you the original message.

✔ Tips

- To reply to all other recipients of an e-mail message as well as the sender, click the Reply All button. You can change or add any e-mail addresses—just be sure to separate multiple addresses with a comma and a space: you@mail.com, me@mail.com.

- To reply to a message you've already read, (or to one you haven't read but you know requires a reply), you can skip opening it first: Click the checkbox to the left of the sender's name in the Inbox message list, then click Reply or Reply All at the bottom of the Inbox page. A message-composition page will open, with the content of the original message quoted in the body of the new message.

- You can add a message's sender to your Address Book by first clicking the message in the Web version of .Mac mail and then clicking the Add Sender button in the toolbar. The sender of the message is added to your .Mac Address Book, and if you use iSync or .Mac Sync, that address will be copied to your other devices as well.

To forward a message:

1. Click the subject line of the message you want to forward.

   The message loads in your Mail window.

2. Click the Forward button (**Figure 2.27**).

   The message-forwarding page opens (**Figure 2.28**).

3. In the To field, enter the e-mail address of the person to whom you want to forward the message.

4. Click the Send button.

   The message is forwarded.

✔ Tip

- To forward a message without opening it first, click the checkbox to the left of the sender's name in the Inbox message list, click Forward at the bottom of the Inbox page, and continue with step 3 above.

Figure 2.27 Click the Forward button to move to .Mac's forward-composition page, where you can write a note at the top of a forwarded e-mail.

Figure 2.28 When you write the introduction to a forwarded message, the original message's text appears below, including some basic e-mail headers (From, To, and so on).

Figure 2.29 To write an e-mail message from scratch, click the Compose button.

Figure 2.30 Blank page—not very inspiring. Here, you enter your recipients' e-mail addresses, a subject, and the text of your message.

- If you want to save a message as a draft while you're working on it, click the Save As Draft button on the message-composition page. The message will be saved in your Drafts folder.

- It's possible to send blind copies of messages using .Mac Webmail. To learn how, see "To add the Bcc field to mail headers" in the "Setting .Mac Mail Preferences" section of this chapter.

To compose and send a message:

1. Log in to your .Mac Webmail account. Your Web browser displays the .Mac e-mail Inbox window.

2. Click the Compose button (**Figure 2.29**). The message-composition page opens (**Figure 2.30**).

3. Enter at least one e-mail address in the To field and as many as you like in the Cc (copy) field.

4. In the Subject field, enter a subject for your message.

5. In the From Address pop-up menu, choose the e-mail address from which you want to send the message (if your .Mac account has more than one address associated with it).

6. In the text box, type the message.

7. In the toolbar at the top of the page, click Send. The e-mail message is sent, and you're returned to the main Mail window.

✔ Tips

- You can check to make sure your e-mail message isn't riddled with misspellings by clicking the Spell Check button before you send. Any misspelled words will be underlined in red, and the number of misspelled words will be shown. Click the Edit link at the bottom to return to the message-composition screen and change the misspelled words.

USING WEBMAIL

To attach a file to a message:

1. Log in to your .Mac Webmail account.

2. Compose a new message to which you want to attach a file.

   The message opens.

3. In the .Mac Webmail toolbar, click the Attach button (**Figure 2.31**).

   The file-attachment page opens (**Figure 2.32**).

4. Click the Choose File button.

   The File Upload sheet slides down (**Figure 2.33**).

Figure 2.31 To attach a file to an outgoing e-mail message, click the Attach button in the toolbar above the composition area.

Figure 2.32 Attaching a file using the file-attachment page is an easy three-step process.

Figure 2.33 Click the Choose File button to open the File Upload window, from which you can choose a file to attach to an e-mail message.

Figure 2.34 Once you've selected a file to be attached, its name shows up in the field to the left of the Browse button.

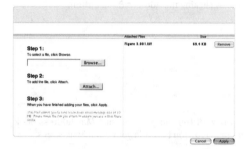

Figure 2.35 Once you've attached a file, it appears in the Attached Files column. You can attach more than one file this way.

Figure 2.36 An attached file appears to the right of the Attachments label, with a nifty paper-clip icon next to it.

5. Navigate to the file that you want to attach to your message, and click Choose.

The name of the file that you chose appears in the field next to the Browse button (**Figure 2.34**).

6. Click the Attach button.

The file is uploaded to the .Mac e-mail servers, and its name appears in the Attached Files column on the right (**Figure 2.35**).

7. Click Apply.

You're returned to the message-composition page, and the name of the file you uploaded appears above the message text area (**Figure 2.36**).

8. Click the Send button.

The message and the attached file are sent, and you're returned to the main Mail window.

✔ Tip

■ To remove an attached file, click the Remove button to the right of the file-name in the message-attachment page as shown in Figure 2.35, or click the disclosure triangle to the right of the Attachments label on the message-composition page as shown in Figure 2.36. Here you can delete attachments and see other information about the files you've uploaded.

Using .Mac's online Address Book

One of the best reasons to have a .Mac account is that .Mac is so well integrated with Mac OS X that it makes tedious tasks less, well, tedious. A good example of this is how .Mac Mail uses e-mail addresses stored in your Address Book. After you've set up synchronization and synced your Address Book to your .Mac account (see Chapter 9, "Using Address Book," for instructions on how to do this), you can easily access all of your e-mail addresses from any Internet-enabled computer, anywhere, anytime. And if you use .Mac's Quick Address feature, entering e-mail addresses can be accomplished with a simple click.

To use an address from Address Book:

1. Log in to your .Mac Webmail account.

2. In the .Mac Webmail toolbar, click the Compose button.

The message-composition page opens.

3. In the .Mac Webmail toolbar, click the Address Book button (**Figure 2.37**).

A page showing the addresses in your online Address Book opens (**Figure 2.38**).

Figure 2.37 Looking for an e-mail address? You can access your Address Book while using .Mac's Webmail by clicking the Address Book button.

Figure 2.38 The addresses in your .Mac Address Book are ready for you to use in your e-mail messages.

Figure 2.39 To include an address in an e-mail message, select To, Cc, or Bcc in the pop-up menu to the right of the address you want to use.

4. From the pop-up menu next to each address, choose the addresses you want to use by selecting To, Cc, or Bcc (**Figure 2.39**).

5. Click the Apply button.

The addresses you selected appear in the appropriate address fields (**Figure 2.40**).

Figure 2.40 The addresses you specified on the Address Book page appear in the appropriate e-mail address fields.

To add an address to the Quick Addresses menu:

1. Log in to your .Mac Webmail account.

   Your Web browser displays your Webmail Inbox page.

2. In the Webmail toolbar, click the Address Book button.

   A page listing addresses in your online Address Book opens. Depending on the number of contacts in your Address Book, you may see only a partial list. If necessary, click the down-arrow button at lower left to view the next page of your list.

3. Check the boxes in the Quick Address column to the right of the addresses that you want to add to the Quick Addresses menu (**Figure 2.41**).

   Cancel and Save buttons appear in the lower-right portion of the page.

4. Click Save.

   The addresses are added to the Quick Addresses menu, available for use when composing an e-mail message.

To use an address from the Quick Addresses menu:

1. Log in to your .Mac Webmail account.

2. In the .Mac Webmail toolbar, click the Compose button.

   The message-composition page opens.

3. To the right of the To, Cc, and Bcc fields, click the Quick Addresses menu to select the address you'd like to add to that field (**Figure 2.42**).

   The address is automatically added to the field (**Figure 2.43**). Repeat as desired to add additional names to each field.

Figure 2.41 To add an address to the Quick Addresses menu, check the box to the right of the address in your online Address Book.

Figure 2.42 Addresses you've selected appear in the Quick Addresses menu, ready and waiting.

Figure 2.43 Once you've chosen an e-mail address from the Quick Addresses menu, it appears in the To, Cc, or Bcc field to its left.

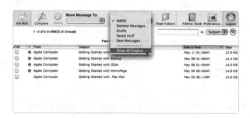

Figure 2.44 From the Go To menu, choose Show All Folders to be taken to a list of your .Mac e-mail folders.

Figure 2.45 You can also click the Show Folders button to see a list of all your .Mac e-mail folders.

Figure 2.46 The Show All Folders view displays all of the folders associated with your .Mac e-mail account.

Working with folders

You can use .Mac Webmail to organize and sort your mail in folders. When you log in to your .Mac e-mail account through a Web browser, you're presented with your Inbox, which is your main folder. Every account also comes with a few additional folders that may show up—Drafts, Sent Messages, and Deleted Messages—and you can create more folders if you like. The Drafts folder appears only after you've saved an e-mail as a draft, and the Sent Messages and Deleted Messages folders appear only if you have the Save Sent Message To and Move Deleted Messages To boxes checked in .Mac Mail preferences.

To view all mail folders:

1. Log in to your .Mac Webmail account.

   Your Web browser displays the Webmail Inbox page.

2. From the Go To pop-up menu, choose Show All Folders (**Figure 2.44**).

   or

   In the .Mac Webmail toolbar, click the Show Folders button (**Figure 2.45**).

   A page opens displaying all of your current e-mail folders, along with each folder's name, the number of unread messages in it, the total number of messages in it, and the size of each folder (**Figure 2.46**).

To create a folder:

1. Log in to your .Mac Webmail account.
   Your Web browser loads the .Mac e-mail
   window.

2. In the .Mac Webmail toolbar, click the
   Show Folders button as shown in
   Figure 2.45.

   A page opens displaying all of your current e-mail folders.

3. In the toolbar at the top of the page, click
   the New button (**Figure 2.47**).

   A new folder appears at the top of your
   current list of e-mail folders.

4. In the folder-name field, type the name
   for your new folder (**Figure 2.48**).

5. Click Save.

   Your new folder is added to your existing
   folder set and appears in your Webmail
   account, as well as in your e-mail client
   (provided you're set up to use your .Mac
   account as an IMAP account).

Figure 2.47 Clicking the New button creates a new
folder in which you can store your e-mail.

Figure 2.48 You can name your folder something useful or memorable—type the name in the field next to
the folder icon and click Save.

Getting Organized

If you have a ton of mail, it's important
to keep it organized—otherwise, you'll
be pushing up against your .Mac data-
storage limit in no time. Here are a few
tips to help you reduce e-mail clutter and
stay within your storage limits.

◆ **Delete what you don't need.** Sure,
   the temptation to keep an e-mail may
   be great, but unless you actually need
   it, get rid of it.

◆ **Set up a group of folders.** And file
   messages in them accordingly.

◆ **Trim attachments when possible.**
   Messages with attached files eat up
   a lot of space, so be sure to download
   the attachments and delete the
   messages.

Figure 2.49 To flag a folder for renaming, check the box to the left of its name.

Figure 2.50 To rename checked folders, click the Rename button.

Figure 2.51 Rename your folder.

To rename a folder:

1. Log in to your .Mac Webmail account.

   Your Web browser loads the .Mac Inbox window.

2. In the .Mac Webmail toolbar, click the Show Folders button.

   A page opens displaying all of your current e-mail folders.

3. Check the boxes next to the folders you want to rename (**Figure 2.49**).

4. In the .Mac Webmail toolbar, click the Rename button (**Figure 2.50**).

   The names of all the checked folders are now editable.

5. Type a new name for each checked folder (**Figure 2.51**).

6. Click Save.

   Your folders should display their new names.

✔ Tips

- You can rename any folder except your Inbox folder.

- You can rename your Drafts and Deleted Messages folders, but resist the urge to do so. If you rename your Drafts folder, you could run into an error the next time you try to save a message. Renaming Deleted Messages seems to work without causing any problems, but it's better to be safe than sorry.

USING WEBMAIL

To delete a folder:

1. Log in to your .Mac Webmail account.
   Your Web browser loads the .Mac Inbox
   window.

2. In the .Mac Webmail toolbar, click the
   Show Folders button.

   A page opens displaying all of your current e-mail folders.

3. Check the boxes next to the folders you
   want to delete (**Figure 2.52**).

4. In the toolbar at the top of the page, click
   the Delete button (**Figure 2.53**).

   A page opens asking if you're sure you
   want to delete the selected folder or folders. If you've selected multiple items,
   you're only warned once (**Figure 2.54**).

5. Click Delete.
   The folder is deleted.

✔ Tips

- To select all the check boxes, click the All
  column header.

- If you delete the Drafts, Sent Messages, or
  Deleted Messages folder, Webmail will re-
  create them automatically the next time
  you save a draft message, send a message,
  or delete one.

Figure 2.52 To flag a folder for deleting, check the box
to the left of its name.

Figure 2.53 Clicking the Delete button deletes all
flagged folders.

Figure 2.54 Before you're allowed to delete a folder,
you're asked if you want to follow through. Click
Delete to continue.

Figure 2.55 To empty a folder, check the box to the left of the folder you want to empty.

Figure 2.56 Click the Empty button in the toolbar to delete all of the messages in the folder.

Deleting all messages in a folder

Sometimes you want to delete all of the messages in a folder but keep the folder itself. Doing so is easy. Here's how.

To delete all messages in a folder:

1. Log in to your .Mac Webmail account.
   Your Web browser loads the .Mac Inbox window.

2. In the .Mac Webmail toolbar, click the Show Folders button, as shown in Figure 2.45.
   A page opens displaying all of your current e-mail folders.

3. Check the box next to the folder you want to empty (**Figure 2.55**).

4. In the toolbar at the top of the page, click Empty (**Figure 2.56**).
   The messages are removed from that folder.

✔ Tip

- When you click the Empty button, you are not asked if you'd like to proceed, so be sure this is really something you want to do before clicking the button.

Emptying the Deleted Messages Folder

When you delete a message, it doesn't actually get deleted. Rather, it gets moved to the Deleted Messages folder, where it awaits its final fate—including a reprieve, if you change your mind. If you don't change your mind, you'll need to empty the Deleted Messages folder.

To empty this folder, choose Show All Folders from the Go To pop-up menu. This loads all available mail folders. To the right of the Deleted Messages item, click the Empty Now link to delete all of your messages for good.

Moving messages

The key to keeping an organized e-mail account is to trash the messages you no longer need and file the messages you want to hold on to for a while. Moving messages between folders is easy.

To move an e-mail message:

1. Log in to your .Mac Webmail account.

   Your Web browser loads the .Mac Inbox window.

2. From the Go To pop-up menu, choose the folder that contains the message you want to move (**Figure 2.57**).

   The folder opens, displaying all of its messages in a list.

3. Check the boxes next to the messages you want to move.

4. From the Move Message To pop-up menu, choose a destination folder for your selected messages (**Figure 2.58**).

   The selected messages are moved to the new folder.

Figure 2.57 From the Go To menu, choose the folder that contains the messages you want to move (or search for); the folder opens on the page.

Figure 2.58 From the Move Message To menu, choose a destination folder for your messages.

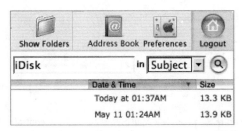

Figure 2.59 Type your search term in the search field.

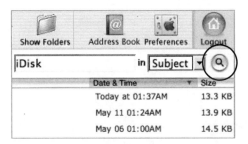

Figure 2.60 To choose what's searched, select Subject, From, To, or CC from the menu.

Figure 2.61 Click the magnifying glass button to perform the search.

Figure 2.62 After you perform a search, the results are shown in a list.

Using search

If you're using your .Mac e-mail account as an IMAP account, you may be storing a lot of messages. Wading through them to find that one special message from the Bulwer-Lytton Fiction Contest, well, it may be daunting when you have 373 messages in your Filed Messages folder, and you can't quite remember the date when the message was sent. That's why your .Mac Web e-mail has a built-in search function.

To find a message using search:

1. Log in to your .Mac Webmail account.
   Your Web browser loads the .Mac Inbox window.

2. From the Go To menu, choose the folder that contains the message you're looking for (see Figure 2.57).
   The folder opens, displaying all of its messages in a list.

3. In the search field in the upper right corner of the page, type the term you want to search for (**Figure 2.59**).

4. From the pop-up menu next to the search field, choose Subject, From, To, or CC (**Figure 2.60**).
   This setting determines whether the program will search message subjects, From addresses, To addresses, or CC addresses.

5. Click the magnifying glass button to the right of the pop-up menu (**Figure 2.61**).
   All messages matching the search term load in a new page (**Figure 2.62**).

✔ Tip

- Search weeds through only one folder at a time. If you have a number of e-mail folders set up, you may have to search each likely folder to find the elusive message.

Setting .Mac Mail Preferences

Now that you know how to read and manage your e-mail using .Mac's Webmail, it's time to set your .Mac e-mail preferences using a Web browser. By doing so, you ensure that your e-mail account behaves the way you want it to. (Wouldn't it be nice if you could do this in other areas of your life . . .)

Your .Mac e-mail preferences are divided into three realms: Viewing, Composing, and Accounts. To access these preferences, log in to your .Mac e-mail account using a Web browser and click the Preferences button. The Viewing and Composing preferences affect only how your .Mac account works when you access it using a Web browser—your Accounts preferences affect how it behaves across the board.

Setting Viewing preferences

The Viewing preferences let you set the time zone, the number of messages displayed in a folder at one time, and whether all e-mail headers are displayed.

To set the time zone:

1. Log in to your .Mac Webmail account.

   Your Web browser loads the .Mac e-mail window.

2. At the top of the window, click the Preferences button (**Figure 2.63**).

   The .Mac e-mail preferences load with the Accounts tab selected as the default (**Figure 2.64**). Don't worry, we'll discuss those options later in the chapter.

Figure 2.63 The .Mac Mail preferences let you control how you see mail, how you write messages, and how your account behaves.

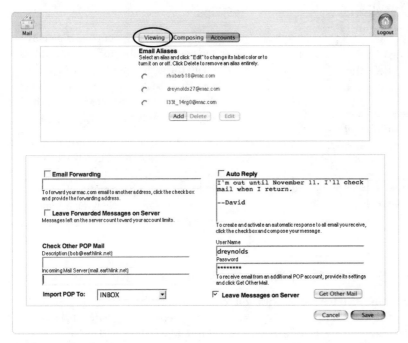

Figure 2.64 Click the Viewing tab at the top of the page to access your Viewing preferences.

Figure 2.65 The .Mac Webmail Viewing preferences let you set your time zone, the number of messages that appear on a given page, and whether all e-mail headers are displayed.

3. Click the Viewing tab at the top of the page.

The Viewing preferences load (**Figure 2.65**).

4. From the Time Zone pop-up menu, choose a location in the time zone you're working in.

5. Click Save.

A message indicating that the change has been saved appears.

To set the number of viewable messages per page:

1. Log in to your .Mac Webmail account and open Viewing preferences.

   The Viewing preferences load.

2. From the Messages Per Page pop-up menu, choose the number of messages you'd like to see on a given page.

3. Click Save.

   Mail shows only the number of messages per page that you've selected.

✔ Tips

■ Ten or 15 messages per page is usually a manageable number for viewing, unless you go through a lot of e-mail in a day—in which case it might be worth listing more. The more messages you list, the longer the scroll.

■ If you want to show all the e-mail headers when you read a message, check the Show "All Headers" Option box on the right side of this page and click Save. Headers let you see where an e-mail has come from, helping you to determine if it's genuine.

Setting .Mac Address Book Preferences

You can control how .Mac Webmail works with your contact information by setting your .Mac Address Book preferences. These preferences govern how contacts are handled and whether syncing is turned on. See Chapter 9 for full details on using Address Book with .Mac.

To get to your .Mac Address Book information, log in to your .Mac account and open your Address Book. Click the Preferences button in the toolbar to load the preferences. Here's what all the settings mean:

◆ **Contacts Per Page.** This setting defaults to displaying 10 contacts per page, but you can set it to 10, 15, 20, 25, 30, or 50. How big is your monitor?

◆ **Display Order.** Sets how contacts are sorted (by first name, last name or last name, first name).

◆ **Default Email.** You can choose which e-mail address—Home or Work—is used as the default address when sending messages.

◆ **Default Phone #1.** Allows you to select which phone is used as default phone number one: Home, Work, Mobile, or Fax.

◆ **Default Phone #2.** Allows you to select which phone is used as default phone number two: Home, Work, Mobile, or Fax.

◆ **Default Sort Order.** Lets you choose how contacts are sorted by default: by e-mail address, last name, or first name.

◆ **Turn on .Mac Address Book Synchronization.** You use this check box to turn on synchronization between your .Mac Address Book and the Address Book on any computer registered with your .Mac account (either via .Mac System Preferences for Mac OS X v10.4 users or via iSync for Mac OS X v10.3 users).

Figure 2.66 When you reply to an HTML e-mail message using a Web browser, the original message is included as an attached file, rather than as text within the message-composition text box.

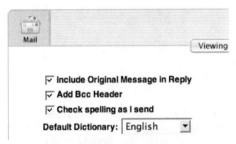

Figure 2.67 The .Mac Webmail Composing preferences let you set what's included in a reply, whether the Bcc header is shown, whether spelling is checked before you send a message, whether a photo or signature is included with a sent message, where sent and deleted messages go, and from whom the message appears to come.

Figure 2.68 Uncheck the top box to prevent inclusion of original message text in your e-mail replies.

Setting Composing preferences

The Composing preferences control what happens when you compose and send an e-mail—everything from whether your original message is included in your reply to how your spelling checker behaves.

To exclude original messages from replies:

By default, whenever you use Webmail to Reply (or Reply All) to a message, the contents of the original message appear in the body of the reply message or as an attachment (if the original e-mail contains complex HTML) (**Figure 2.66**). If you don't like this, you aren't forever condemned to erase repeated content. Here's how to turn off that behavior:

1. Log in to your .Mac Webmail preferences.
   The .Mac e-mail preferences load.

2. Click the Composing tab.
   The Composing preferences load (**Figure 2.67**).

3. In the upper left corner of the page, uncheck the Include Original Message in Reply box (**Figure 2.68**).

4. Click Save.

To add the Bcc field to mail headers:

The blind-carbon-copy (Bcc) address field lets you send copies of a message to someone without letting other recipients know that person is receiving a copy.

1. On the Composing tab of your .Mac e-mail preferences, check the Add Bcc Header box (**Figure 2.69**).

2. Click Save.

   The Bcc header appears in all .Mac Webmail messages (**Figure 2.70**).

✔ Tip

■ Besides its many uses in the realm of office politics, the Bcc field is handy for forwarding the latest e-mail joke or cartoon to your friends: If you address the message to yourself in the To field and put all other addresses in the Bcc field, you'll spare your friends from seeing all the other recipients' addresses when they open the message.

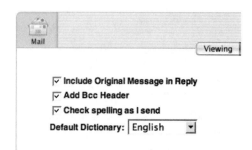

Figure 2.69 Check the Add Bcc Header box to have the Bcc header included in e-mail messages you write.

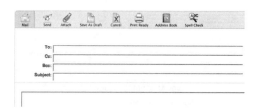

Figure 2.70 The Bcc header appears in Webmail messages if the proper preference is set, allowing blind-carbon-copy recipients to be added to a message.

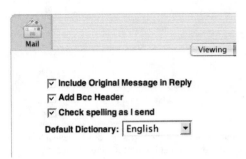

Figure 2.71 Check the last box to have your message's spelling checked when you send it.

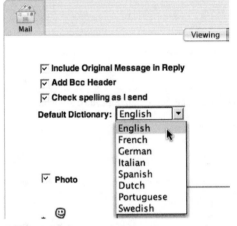

Figure 2.72 From this menu, you can choose the language in which you'd like your e-mail's spelling checked.

Figure 2.73 .Mac's built-in spelling checker shows you words that it suspects are misspelled and provides alternatives.

To have spelling checked before sending:

1. On the Composing tab of your .Mac e-mail preferences, check the "Check spelling as I send" box (**Figure 2.71**).

2. From the Default Dictionary pop-up menu, choose a language (**Figure 2.72**).

3. Click Save.

   Mail checks spelling before you send your message, using the language you've selected for your default dictionary (**Figure 2.73**).

To create an automatic signature:

A mail signature is a block of text that appears at the bottom of every e-mail message you compose. It typically contains the sender's name, address, and other contact information. Some folks also include a favorite quote, a link to their Homepage, or what have you. Here's how to make your own:

1. On the Composing tab of your .Mac e-mail preferences, check the Signature box (**Figure 2.74**).

2. In the text box below the Signature check box, type the text you'd like to use as your signature (**Figure 2.75**).

3. Click Save.

   Your new signature appears at the bottom of each .Mac Webmail message you send (**Figure 2.76**).

✔ Tip

■ If you're using your .Mac e-mail account for business purposes, include your name, address, phone number, and Website address in your signature to help customers contact you easily. And even though addressees can easily click Reply to respond to your message, include your e-mail address as well, in case a recipient prints your message and wants to reply later.

Figure 2.74 Check the Signature box to have a text signature placed at the bottom of each message you send through .Mac's Webmail.

Figure 2.75 Enter the signature you'd like to have appear on e-mails that you send.

Figure 2.76 When composing a message using the signature option, the signature appears in the message-composition area automatically.

Figure 2.77 Check the Photo box to have a photo included with each message you send through .Mac's Webmail.

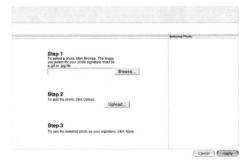

Figure 2.78 On this page, you can choose an image using the Browse button.

Figure 2.79 In the File Upload window, you can find and select an image to upload.

To add an image to your Webmail reply:

This task adds an image to messages that you send through .Mac Webmail—it's not for sending an image as an attachment.

1. On the Composing tab of your .Mac Mail preferences, check the Photo box (**Figure 2.77**).

2. Click Choose.

   A page opens where you can choose an image (**Figure 2.78**).

3. Click the Browse button.

   The File Upload sheet slides down (**Figure 2.79**).

4. Navigate to the image you want to use in your message and click Open.

   The File Upload window closes, returning you to your preferences page.

   continues on next page

SETTING .MAC MAIL PREFERENCES

5. Back on the image-selection page, the name of the image you selected appears in the Step 1 field (**Figure 2.80**). Click the Upload button.

The image is uploaded to your .Mac account.

6. Click the Apply button.

The preferences page opens with the Composing tab selected.

7. Click Save.

When you send a .Mac Webmail message, the image you selected automatically appears in the upper right corner of your message (**Figure 2.81**).

Other Composing Preferences

Additional settings options found in the upper-right portion of the Composing preferences page allow you to *do any of the following (see Figure 2.68):*

▲ Check the Save Sent Messages To box to have messages that you send saved. Choose the folder in which you want to have these messages saved from the pop-up menu.

▲ Check the Move Deleted Messages To box to have messages that you delete moved to the folder you select in the pop-up menu.

▲ To set the name that appears in the From line of the messages you send, type a new one in the field titled From (Your Name).

✔ Tips

■ To remove a custom image or icon, click the Remove button on the Composing preferences page, and click Save.

■ If you're using your .Mac e-mail for business, you can use the photo feature to add a company logo to your Webmail messages.

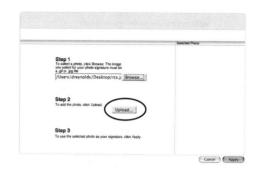

Figure 2.80 Click the Upload button to upload the selected item to the .Mac servers.

Figure 2.81 Your image appears in the upper right corner of all .Mac e-mails sent using Webmail.

Setting Accounts preferences

Although you must log in to your .Mac account on the Web to access the Accounts preferences, they affect how your .Mac account works both online and on your Desktop. The Accounts preferences enable you to create e-mail aliases, edit existing aliases—which essentially means that you can make them inactive or change the color of the messages that come in to the aliases—forward your mail, set up an auto reply, and set .Mac to check other e-mail accounts you might have.

Aliases, if you've never used them before, are e-mail addresses that don't have accounts associated with them. Mail sent to an alias is redirected to another address—one with an associated account. If your account was me@mac.com, for example, you could create an alias called myalias@mac.com, and all e-mail to myalias@mac.com would be automatically delivered to me@mac.com. Why do this? You can give out aliased e-mail addresses without fear—if an alias is abused (with, say, a forklift full of spam), simply delete it and create a new alias. Your original e-mail address remains uncompromised.

Using Accounts preferences, you can also set up your .Mac e-mail account so that all messages that come to it are forwarded to another e-mail account. This is useful if, for example, you won't be checking your .Mac e-mail account, and you want someone else to be able to read the messages while you're away. Simply forward the messages to that person's e-mail address, and every message sent to your .Mac account will be redirected to that person's account.

Printing a Message

If you're reading a message you simply must have in paper form, you can print it in a format that your printer is more likely to appreciate—or at least one that doesn't require so much paper and ink. Open the message that you want to print, and click the Print Ready button. A new window will open that contains the e-mail headers and text—with no extraneous graphics. From the File menu, choose Print to open the Print dialog, where you'll choose Print again.

To create an e-mail alias:

1. Log in to your .Mac Webmail preferences. The .Mac e-mail preferences load.

2. Click the Accounts tab.
   The Accounts preferences load (**Figure 2.82**).

3. In the Email Aliases section at the top of the page, click the Create Alias button.
   The page for creating a new e-mail alias opens (**Figure 2.83**).

4. In the text field, type an e-mail alias (it can't have any spaces or other non-alphanumeric characters, or it won't work) (**Figure 2.84**).

5. Click the radio button next to the color you'd like to assign to messages sent to that alias (Figure 2.84). The color you choose affects only the listing in your inbox (the From and Subject text for example); it doesn't affect the way mail you send appears to the recipient(s).

6. Click the Create Alias button.
   The new e-mail alias is now ready. You can send e-mail to that alias (with *@mac.com* at the end, as in myname54@mac.com), and it will arrive in your main .Mac Inbox.

✔ Tip

- You can have up to five aliases at a time on a given .Mac account. If you have five aliases and you delete one, you'll have to wait seven days before you can create a new alias.

Figure 2.82 The .Mac Mail Accounts preferences let you create and manage e-mail aliases, forward e-mail, check other e-mail accounts, and set an automatic reply.

Figure 2.83 The e-mail alias page allows you to create an e-mail alias and choose a color for mail sent to that alias.

Figure 2.84 Type a word or phrase that you'd like to use for an alias—but remember, you can't use spaces or other non-alphanumeric characters.

Figure 2.85 To edit or delete an e-mail alias, click the radio button to the left of the alias, and then click the Edit or Delete button.

Figure 2.86 On the alias-editing page, you can choose a color for an alias or set whether or not an alias is active.

Figure 2.87 Click the radio button next to the e-mail alias you want to delete.

Figure 2.88 Click the Delete button to delete the alias.

To edit an existing alias:

1. On the Accounts tab of your .Mac Webmail preferences, click the radio button next to the alias that you want to edit (**Figure 2.85**).

   The Edit button becomes active.

2. Click the Edit button.

   The alias-editing page opens (**Figure 2.86**).

3. *Do one of the following:*

   ▲ To turn on an alias, click the Active radio button.

   ▲ To turn off an alias, click the Inactive radio button.

   ▲ To change the color of messages arriving at that alias, click the radio button next to your preferred color.

4. Click Save.

   The changes to your alias take effect immediately.

To delete an existing alias:

1. On the Accounts tab of your .Mac Webmail preferences, click the radio button next to the alias that you want to delete (**Figure 2.87**).

   The Delete button becomes active.

2. Click the Delete button.

   A new page opens asking if you're sure you want to delete the alias (**Figure 2.88**).

3. Click Delete.

   The alias is deleted from your account and cannot be reused.

✔ Tip

■ Remember: Once you delete an e-mail alias, it can't be reused, so be sure this is something you want to do.

SETTING .MAC MAIL PREFERENCES

To forward all of your .Mac mail:

There may be times (when you're on vacation, for instance) when it's useful to route mail from your .Mac account to another mail account (that of a co-worker, perhaps). Here's how to do that:

1. On the Accounts tab of your .Mac Webmail preferences, check the Email Forwarding box (**Figure 2.89**).

2. In the text box below the Email Forwarding check box, type the e-mail address to which you want the messages forwarded.

3. Click Save.

   Your messages are forwarded to the account you specified until you turn off mail forwarding.

✔ Tip

■ If you want to leave the forwarded messages in your .Mac e-mail account, be sure to check the Leave Forwarded Messages on Server box. To retrieve these messages later, simply connect to your .Mac account with your e-mail client and check your mail as you normally would.

To set up an auto reply:

If you'll be unable to answer mail from your .Mac account for a while, here's how you can set up an automatic response message, letting people who send you mail know you're away, and when you'll be back in action:

1. On the Accounts tab of your .Mac Webmail preferences, check the Auto Reply box (**Figure 2.90**).

2. In the text box below the Auto Reply check box, type the message that you want to have sent as your auto reply.

3. Click Save.

   Your automatic reply is sent to everyone who sends you an e-mail message.

Figure 2.89 Check the Email Forwarding box and provide an e-mail address as the destination for forwarded mail, if you want your .Mac e-mail to arrive in another e-mail inbox.

Figure 2.90 Anyone who sends a message to your .Mac e-mail address will receive the text you type into the Auto Reply text box as a reply.

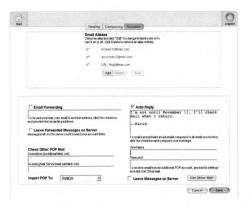

Figure 2.91 Filling in the relevant fields enables you to check other e-mail accounts and import that mail into your .Mac e-mail Inbox.

Figure 2.92 Your incoming-mail-server address (with a short description of the account) is key to checking another e-mail account.

Figure 2.93 Provide the user name and password to check e-mail from another account.

To check other e-mail accounts:

Here's how you can use .Mac Webmail to check e-mail from other (non-.Mac) mail accounts. (Note that this works only with POP mail accounts; IMAP accounts typically require you to use their own Webmail-style interfaces to get messages.)

1. On the Accounts tab of your .Mac Webmail preferences, scroll down to the Check Other POP Mail section (**Figure 2.91**).

2. In the Description field, type the e-mail address of the account you want to check.

3. In the Incoming Mail Server field, enter the name of the incoming mail server for the account you want to check (**Figure 2.92**).

4. In the UserName field, enter the member name of your account (**Figure 2.93**). Typically, the user name is the first part of the e-mail address, before the @ symbol. Check with the service provider that handles that particular e-mail address to be sure.

continues on next page

SETTING .MAC MAIL PREFERENCES

5. In the Password field, enter the password of the account you want to check. All e-mail accounts have associated passwords (or they should). This is what you typed when you first set up your e-mail account; if you're not sure what this is, check with the service provider that handles that particular e-mail address.

6. Check the Leave Messages on Server box if you want the messages to remain on the other mail server for later pickup (**Figure 2.94**).

7. Click the Get Other Mail button.

After a short delay, any mail waiting in the other account is imported into the Inbox of .Mac's Webmail.

Figure 2.94 Check this box to ensure that messages are left on the original mail server.

✔ Tip

■ Once you're done working with your e-mail, you'll want to log out of your .Mac account. To do so, simply click your user name in the Log Out area on the right side of the toolbar or click the Logout button in the Mail toolbar (either of which logs you out of your .Mac account).

Figure 2.95 Click the iCards link in the toolbar to be taken to the main iCards page.

Figure 2.96 On the Compose/Edit page, you can create your own custom iCard.

About iCards

iCards aren't part of your .Mac e-mail account, but they work closely with it. Your .Mac account comes with hundreds of high-quality electronic greeting cards that you can send to anyone via e-mail. There are a number of categories to choose from (just like going into your own Hallmark store), including seasonal, birthdays, romance, and get well. If you're feeling extra-creative, you can send a custom iCard—one that contains your own pictures—rather than using one of the prefab pictures.

To send an iCard:

1. Go to www.mac.com and log in to your .Mac account.

   The main .Mac page opens.

2. In the toolbar at the top of the page, click the iCards link (**Figure 2.95**).

   The iCards page opens.

3. Click the card you want to send to select it. You can choose from a large number of categories on the left, and then you can browse through the various cards in a category.

   The Compose/Edit page opens (**Figure 2.96**).

continues on next page

ABOUT iCARDS

4. Click the radio button next to the font you want to use.

5. In the message text field, type your message (**Figure 2.97**). The message will appear in boring plain text, but the font you picked will appear in the copy the recipient sees.

6. Click the Continue button in the lower right corner of the page.

The Address & Send page opens with the name and e-mail address associated with your .Mac account already entered in the appropriate fields (**Figure 2.98**).

7. In the "Enter your name" field, type your name if the information that's already entered is incorrect.

8. In the "Enter your email" field, type your e-mail address if the information that's already entered is incorrect.

Figure 2.97 Type the message you want to send in the text box.

Figure 2.98 Enter your name and address information on the Address & Send page if it hasn't been automatically filled in correctly.

Figure 2.99 Type the e-mail addresses to which you want to send the card in the "Enter emails, separated by commas" field.

Figure 2.100 Check the boxes for the addresses from your Address Book to which you want to send the iCard.

9. *Do one or more of the following:*

   ▲ From the ".Mac members select from your Address Book" pop-up menu, choose the e-mail addresses to which you want to send the card from your Quick Addresses list.

   ▲ In the "Enter emails, separated by commas" text box, type the e-mail addresses to which you want to send the card (**Figure 2.99**). If you want to send the card to more than one e-mail address, separate multiple addresses by commas.

   ▲ Click the Address Book button to select e-mail addresses from your .Mac Address Book. Check the boxes next to the addresses you want to use, and then click Return to Card (**Figure 2.100**).

continues on next page

10. In the upper right corner of the page, click the Send Card button (**Figure 2.101**).

The card is sent to the e-mail addresses you've specified, and you're given a hearty congratulations on a job well done (**Figure 2.102**).

✔ Tips

■ To view all of the card styles before making your selection, click Browse All Cards at the bottom of the iCards Categories list on the main iCards page.

■ To have a copy of the iCard sent to you as well, check the "Send myself a copy" box before sending the card.

■ If you want the people to whom you're sending the card to be unable to see who else received it, check the "Hide distribution list" box.

Figure 2.101 Click the Send Card button to send the iCard.

Figure 2.102 Nice work—you've sent an iCard!

Figure 2.103 The Create Your Own link is your key to making a custom iCard.

Figure 2.104 When you select an image from your iDisk for an iCard, a preview appears on the right.

Figure 2.105 On the Compose/Edit page you can add custom text to your custom card.

To send a custom iCard:

1. Go to www.mac.com and log in to your .Mac account.

   The main .Mac page opens.

2. In the toolbar at the top of the page, click the iCards link.

   The iCards page opens.

3. In the iCards Categories list on the right, click Create Your Own (**Figure 2.103**).

   The "Select an image" page opens. The column on the left shows the contents of your iDisk's Pictures folder.

4. From the left column, click the name of an image to select it.

   A preview of the image opens on the right (**Figure 2.104**).

5. Click the Select This Image button.

   The Compose/Edit page opens (**Figure 2.105**).

6. Click the radio button next to the font you want to use.

7. In the message text box, type your message.

8. Check the "Resize your image to fit card" box to trim the image to proper size.

9. Click the Continue button.

   The Address & Send page opens with the name and e-mail address associated with your .Mac account already entered in the appropriate fields.

10. In the "Enter your name" field, type your name if the information that's already entered is incorrect.

11. In the "Enter your email" field, type your e-mail address if the information that's already entered is incorrect.

continues on next page

ABOUT iCARDS

12. *Do one or more of the following:*

▲ From the ".Mac members select from your Address Book" pop-up menu, choose an e-mail address.

▲ In the "Enter emails, separated by commas" field, type an e-mail address.

▲ Click the Address Book button to select an e-mail address from your .Mac Address Book. Check the boxes next to the addresses you want to use, and then click Return to Card.

13. Click the Send Card button.

The card is sent to the e-mail addresses you've specified.

Contributing to the Members Portfolio

Your .Mac account lets you show off your digital photography by contributing to the .Mac Members Portfolio. Here's how you can submit your art for consideration:

1. Save your pictures as JPEG images, and make sure the filenames end with either the .jpg or .jpeg file extension.

2. Make sure that filenames contain only uppercase letters, lowercase letters, numbers, and the underscore character. Other characters won't work.

3. Make sure the pictures are larger than 312 by 416 pixels.

4. Move the pictures you're submitting to the Pictures folder on your iDisk.

5. Log in to your .Mac account, click the iCards link, and then click the Members Portfolio link. Follow the onscreen instructions to submit your artwork, which will then be judged by .Mac officials—not every image gets selected.

3

USING IDISK

Network storage of one kind or another has been around for decades. Back in the day, if you wanted to move files to a file server, your computer had to be connected to the same network as that file server. If your computer wasn't physically linked to that server, you couldn't connect—and you used the good ol' sneakernet file transfer.

The Internet changed all that by allowing different kinds of computers running different kinds of operating systems to connect to each other around the world. Thanks to the Internet, you can access files stored online from just about anywhere.

iDisk is a .Mac utility that lets you store your files on servers maintained by Apple. These servers house files for thousands of .Mac subscribers. When one of those subscribers connects to his or her iDisk using a Mac, the iDisk appears on the Desktop as if it were a network volume on a file server sitting in a closet down the hall. Users can treat the iDisk almost as if it were a hard drive connected directly to their Macs. And you don't have to use a Mac to do it—most Windows PCs can get at an iDisk with little trouble.

In this chapter, I'll cover how to use your iDisk—how to connect to it, how to copy files to it, and how to use the folders stored on it.

About iDisk

Your .Mac account comes with 1 GB of online storage that you can divide between your iDisk and your .Mac Mail account. When divvying up storage capacity, however, keep in mind that your 1GB of iDisk space also serves as storage for a slew of .Mac services, including Backup, iCal, Sync, .Mac Slides Publisher, Groups, HomePage, iWeb, iPhoto, iMovie, and iCards.

In fact, your iDisk comes populated with several folders, some of which already contain files (**Figure 3.1**). You'll find the folder structure familiar—it's similar to the one in Mac OS X's home folder. Here's a look at what each folder is for and what's in each one (if anything).

Figure 3.1 Your iDisk comes with several folders already on it. Some of these folders are empty, and some contain files (such as software from Apple and files you may have put there through HomePage, iWeb, Backup, or Sync).

◆ **Backup.** This folder is used by the Backup software that comes with your .Mac subscription. If you haven't used Backup, this folder will hold just one file that explains the purpose of the folder. If you have used Backup, the files you've chosen to back up will be here. The folder is read-only—that is, you can view the files and download them to your hard disk, but you can't upload anything into the folder. That's something only Backup can do.

◆ **Documents.** This is a convenient place to hold your various documents if you need to access them online. It's also a good place to back up important documents (although Backup can take care of this for you).

◆ **Groups.** This folder holds the files associated with any groups that you create. (See Chapter 7 for more on .Mac Groups.)

ABOUT IDISK

◆ **Library.** This folder may or may not exist for you, depending on whether you've used an application that uses .Mac. The Library folder isn't really for your use— rather, it's a place where applications that work with .Mac can store their own data. You can browse this folder, but since there's nothing really useful here, it's probably best to just leave well enough alone.

◆ **Movies.** You can store movies you want to share in this folder. Movies in this folder are available to HomePage so that you can easily create Web pages with them. If you create a movie page with iWeb, those movies are located in the Web folder instead. (HomePage is covered in Chapter 4, and Chapter 5 is all about iWeb.)

◆ **Music.** You can use the Music folder to store music. If you create a page with music or sound files using iWeb, those files are stored in the Web folder instead.

◆ **Pictures.** This folder (as its name implies) is where you store digital photos and other pictures. Pictures in this folder are made available to HomePage for publishing photo galleries and to iCards for sending custom iCards. If you create a page with photos using iWeb, those photos are stored in the Web folder instead.

◆ **Public.** The Public folder is meant for sharing files with others. You can put anything in it that you like, and others can download those files at will (depending on how you have your Public folder set up).

◆ **Sites.** The Sites folder is where you store Web pages for others to view when they connect to your .Mac Web site. When you use HomePage on .Mac, it creates HTML files and the folders to hold them here as

continues on next page

ABOUT IDISK

well. If you've created a site using iWeb, those site pages are stored in the Sites folder nested in the Web folder.

◆ **Software.** The Software folder is divided into two parts: Apple Software and Members Only. The contents of these folders consist of downloadable bits of software, all for your use, and they don't count toward your iDisk storage limit. The Apple Software folder has software updates and other Apple-made utilities; the Members Only folder contains special downloads for .Mac members, such as games, third-party utilities, and music. You can download from this folder, but you can't upload to it.

◆ **Web.** The Web folder is reserved for iWeb. It contains all of the HTML files, movie files, image, files, and sound files used to create and upload a Web page using iWeb.

How to Choose Allocation Amounts

Your .Mac account comes with 1 GB of space, which you can divide between your iDisk and your e-mail account. How should you divvy up this space?

It really depends on how you use your e-mail.

If you use POP as your e-mail protocol, you probably don't need a lot of storage space for e-mail, so you can set it for 15 MB or so, and see how that works. Remember, with POP, when you connect to your e-mail account, you download all of your mail to your computer, freeing up that space.

If you use IMAP as your e-mail protocol, you should start with something beefier, depending on how much mail you intend to store. Try allocating 125 MB for e-mail, and if you're bumping up against the limit in your e-mail, give it more space. If, after a month or so, you find that you're not using all of that space, you can reduce your allocation.

In the end, it's not critical how you divvy up this space—after all, if you run out of e-mail space or iDisk space, you can always reallocate how the space is used. And if you really need to stretch out, you can always purchase an extra gig of storage for $49.95 per year (or three more gigs for $99.95 per year).

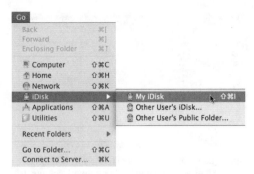

Figure 3.2 Since iDisk access is built into recent versions of Mac OS X, connecting to your iDisk is as easy as choosing Go > iDisk > My iDisk (Command-Shift-I).

Figure 3.3 To connect to your iDisk (if you haven't entered your iDisk information in System Preferences), enter your .Mac member name and password, and click Connect.

Connecting to Your iDisk

If you're using Mac OS X, there are a few ways of connecting to your iDisk, depending on what version of Mac OS X you're running. If you're using Mac OS 9, you'll need additional software to connect to your iDisk (see the sidebar "When David Met Goliath," later in this chapter). Your iDisk uses a network protocol called WebDAV, which simply means that it uses some of the same kinds of connections you'd use to load a Web page in a browser. Since WebDAV is a cross-platform protocol, you can connect to your iDisk using a Macs running Mac OS X and Mac OS 9, as well as a Windows machines running Windows XP, Windows 2000, or Windows 98.

Windows XP uses an Apple-created utility to connect to an iDisk; you can download it from your .Mac account. The utility is somewhat similar to Goliath, except that it requires more work to install. Windows 2000, however, has built-in support for connecting to WebDAV-based online storage accounts (much like Mac OS X), and it does not need Goliath to do the job.

To connect to iDisk using Mac OS X v10.3 or later:

1. From the Go menu, choose iDisk > My iDisk (Command-Shift-I) (**Figure 3.2**).

   If you've already entered your .Mac member name and password in System Preferences, your iDisk mounts automatically on your Desktop. Otherwise, the Connect To iDisk dialog opens, asking for that information (**Figure 3.3**).

   continues on next page

2. Enter your .Mac member name and password, and click Connect.

Your iDisk, which looks like a small globe with your .Mac member name underneath it, mounts on your Desktop, and you can use it like any other volume using a Finder window (**Figure 3.4**). The connection to your iDisk is maintained until you disconnect it or shut down your computer.

✔ Tips

■ You can also click the iDisk icon in the sidebar of a Finder window (Figure 3.4) to connect to your iDisk, if you've already entered your .Mac information in System Preferences.

■ Connecting to an iDisk with a slow or high-latency Internet link can be very trying. If you're using dial-up or satellite to get to the Internet, be sure that no one else (and no other application on your Mac) is using the connection before you connect to your iDisk.

■ If you're using a version of Mac OS X earlier than 10.3, you can still connect to your iDisk by choosing Go > iDisk and entering your .Mac member name and password. After you do that, your iDisk will mount on your Desktop.

■ Remember—you remain connected to your iDisk until you disconnect or shut down. To disconnect your iDisk, drag its icon to the Trash.

Figure 3.4 Once you've connected to your iDisk, you can use it as you would any other network volume. It shows up in the sidebar and on the Desktop, and you can browse it using any view—list, icon, or column.

When David Met Goliath

Figure 3.5 The cutely named homepage for Goliath contains links to Mac OS 9 and Mac OS X versions of the Goliath WebDAV application, as well as some valuable WebDAV information.

Figure 3.6 When you decompress Goliath, a simple disk-image file icon appears on your Desktop.

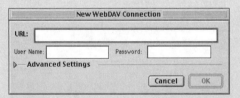

Figure 3.7 You can use this dialog to make a WebDAV connection, but Goliath has a better way to connect to an iDisk.

A third-party program called Goliath makes it possible for you to connect to your iDisk using Mac OS 9, which is handy if you haven't yet upgraded to Mac OS X.

To connect to your iDisk using Mac OS 9:

1. Using a Web browser, go to www.webdav.org/goliath and download Goliath, created by Tom Bednarz (**Figure 3.5**). The software downloads to your hard drive in the form of a compressed file. You'll find it wherever your browser normally downloads files (often, that's on the Desktop).

2. Double-click the compressed Goliath file to decompress it using Allume Systems's StuffIt Expander.

   A disk-image file appears on your Desktop, or wherever you normally download files (**Figure 3.6**).

3. Mount the disk image by double-clicking it, and then copy Goliath to your Mac's Applications (Mac OS 9) folder.

4. Double-click the Goliath program icon to run Goliath.

   The New WebDAV Connection dialog opens and asks you to enter some WebDAV information (**Figure 3.7**).

5. Click Cancel—we'll be taking a different approach to connecting.

   The dialog closes.

continues on next page

CONNECTING TO YOUR IDISK

(continued)

6. From the File menu, choose Open iDisk Connection (**Figure 3.8**).

   The Open an iDisk Connection dialog opens (**Figure 3.9**).

7. Enter your .Mac member name and password (**Figure 3.10**).

8. Click OK.

   Your iDisk opens in a new Goliath window that looks significantly like a Finder window (**Figure 3.11**).

Besides making it possible for Mac OS 9 machines to connect to an iDisk, Goliath is a slick utility developed to allow Mac OS 9 and Mac OS X users to take advantage of WebDAV online storage accounts in a friendly and Mac-like way. It's especially good for the following:

- It allows you to connect to other WebDAV-based online storage accounts, so if you have a WebDAV-based account in addition to your iDisk, you can use the same program to access them both.

- It works very well with high-latency connections (such as satellite Internet), so if regular iDisk performance in Mac OS X seems sluggish, try using Goliath as an alternative.

Figure 3.8 From Goliath's File menu, choose Open iDisk Connection to open a connection to your iDisk.

Figure 3.9 When you use Goliath to request an iDisk connection, you'll be asked for your .Mac member name and password.

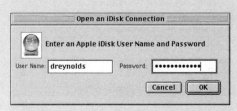

Figure 3.10 Type your .Mac member name in the User Name field and type your password in the Password field. Click OK.

Figure 3.11 Once you've made your connection using Goliath, you're presented with an iDisk window that looks almost exactly like a Finder window.

Figure 3.12 iDisk Utility for Windows is available for download from the .Mac Member Central page.

Figure 3.13 Once downloaded, iDisk Utility for Windows appears in its compressed form.

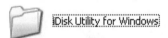

Figure 3.14 iDisk Utility for Windows, once uncompressed, resides in its own folder.

Figure 3.15 The first step when installing iDisk Utility for Windows XP is to read the welcome and copyright warning message.

To connect to iDisk using Windows XP:

1. Using a Web browser, log in to your .Mac account and download iDisk Utility for Windows XP from the Member Centeral page (iDiskUtility_WindowsXP.zip) (**Figure 3.12**).

   The file downloads to your hard drive, but it's compressed, so you'll need to decompress it before you can install it.

2. Unzip iDisk Utility (**Figure 3.13**).

   The iDisk Utility installer is decompressed, and a folder that contains it appears in the location where you normally download files, ready for installation (**Figure 3.14**).

3. Install iDisk Utility for Windows by double-clicking the iDisk Utility installer icon.

   The welcome pane opens.

4. Read the welcome message and copyright warning, and then click Next (**Figure 3.15**).

   The license agreement opens.

continues on next page

5. After reading the license agreement, click the I Agree radio button and then click Next (**Figure 3.16**).

6. If the default installation location is acceptable, click Next (**Figure 3.17**). The Confirm Installation pane opens.

7. To begin the installation, click Next (**Figure 3.18**).

The Installing iDisk Utility for Windows pane opens, and a progress bar shows the installation of the software. It takes only a short time—less than a minute—and you don't have to do anything during the process.

Figure 3.17 When installing iDisk Utility for Windows, you're given a default installation location and the option to install it for everyone who uses the computer or just for yourself. The default settings are fine for most people; feel free to change them if you need to.

Figure 3.16 To proceed with the installation, read the license agreement and click the I Agree radio button.

Figure 3.18 Click Next in the Confirm Installation pane to install iDisk Utility for Windows XP.

Figure 3.19 Choose Start > All Programs > .Mac Utilities > iDisk Utility for Windows > iDisk Utilty for Windows.

Figure 3.20 To connect to an iDisk using iDisk Utility for Windows XP, you'll need to enter your .Mac member name in the "iDisk account" field, enter your password in the Password field, and choose the drive to which your iDisk gets mounted.

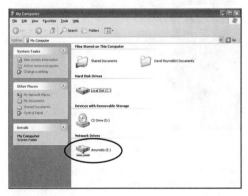

Figure 3.21 Once mounted, your iDisk appears like any other network drive in your My Computer window.

8. When the Installation Complete pane appears, click the Close button.

   iDisk Utility for Windows XP has been installed and is ready to use.

9. From the Start menu, choose All Programs > .Mac Utilities > iDisk Utility for Windows > iDisk Utility for Windows (**Figure 3.19**).

   iDisk Utility opens, and the iDisk Utility for XP login dialog opens (**Figure 3.20**).

10. In the "iDisk account" field, enter your .Mac member name.

11. In the Password field, enter your .Mac password.

12. Select the iDisk radio button.

13. From the Drive pop-up menu, choose a drive to which to mount your iDisk.

14. Click the Mount iDisk button.

    Your iDisk is mounted as a network drive (**Figure 3.21**).

✔ Tips

■ Windows may give you a warning stating that it can't identify who created the installer, but this is OK—it's simply a security measure to keep you from installing any bad software, and if you've downloaded the software from Apple's site, you're safe. Follow the installer's instructions.

■ The first time you run the utility, Windows will tell you that iDisk Utility will modify something called the Hosts file—part of Windows that looks up servers across the Internet. This is OK.

CONNECTING TO YOUR iDISK

To connect using Windows 2000:

1. Double-click the My Computer icon.

   The My Computer window opens (**Figure 3.22**).

2. From the Tools menu, choose Map Network Drive (**Figure 3.23**).

   The Map Network Drive dialog opens.

3. At the bottom of the dialog, click "Create a shortcut to a Web folder or FTP site" (**Figure 3.24**).

   The Add Network Place Wizard dialog opens (**Figure 3.25**).

Figure 3.22 In Windows 2000, you'll need to open a new window to access the Tools menu. Here, we've chosen to do this from the My Computer window, but it can be done from just about any window, such as the My Documents window.

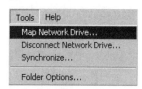

Figure 3.23 From the Tools menu in Windows 2000, choose Map Network Drive to connect to your iDisk.

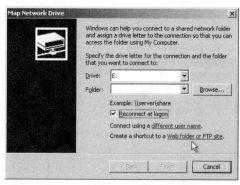

Figure 3.24 Near the bottom of the Map Network Drive dialog, click "Create a shortcut to a Web folder or FTP site."

Connecting to Someone Else's Public Folder Using Mac OS 9

Remember Goliath, the little utility that could? (If not, see the sidebar "When David met Goliath," earlier in this chapter.) Mixed-up metaphors aside, you can also use Goliath to connect to someone else's Public folder when you're running Mac OS 9.

Simply run Goliath by double-clicking its icon and typing http://idisk.mac.com/ *membername*-Public, replacing *member-name* with the member name for the Public folder to which you're connecting. Note that the "P" in Public must be capitalized for this URL to work.

If a password has been set for the Public folder, type public in the User Name field, and the password that was set for the Public folder in the Password field.

The Public folder opens in a new Goliath window, and you can upload and download files to and from it.

CONNECTING TO YOUR iDISK

Figure 3.25 In the opening pane of the Add Network Place Wizard, type your iDisk URL (which looks like http://idisk.mac.com/*membername*, replacing *membername* with your .Mac member name).

Figure 3.26 This is what a properly formed iDisk URL should look like. This one, of course, is the one I use to connect to my iDisk, so it won't work so well for you.

Figure 3.27 To set up the connection to your iDisk, you need to provide your .Mac member name and password in the "User name" and Password fields, respectively.

4. In the field labeled "Type the location of the Network Place," type `http://idisk.mac.com/`*membername* (replacing *membername* with your .Mac member name), and click Next (**Figure 3.26**).

   The Enter Network Password dialog opens.

5. In the "User name" and Password fields, enter your .Mac member name and password, and click OK (**Figure 3.27**).

   The Add Network Place Wizard dialog opens, asking you to name your new Network Place—Windows fills this in for you.

   continues on next page

6. If you don't like the Network Place name that Windows provided, type a new name for your Network Place (such as *My iDisk*), and click Finish (**Figure 3.28**).

Your iDisk opens in a new window (**Figure 3.29**).

✔ Tips

■ You can use the same steps to connect to someone else's iDisk, provided you know his or her member name and password.

■ To access your iDisk later, open My Network Places from the Windows desktop, and your saved iDisk location will appear in a new window. Double-click it to open your iDisk.

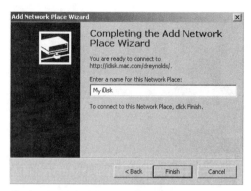

Figure 3.28 The final thing you need to do when creating your iDisk connection is to give it a name. This is the name that will appear under the icon in your My Network Places folder.

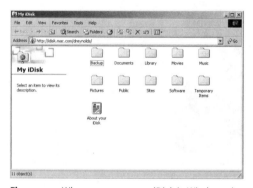

Figure 3.29 When you open your iDisk in Windows, it looks very much like any other storage device, complete with files and folders.

Buying More iDisk Storage

So, you've outgrown the relatively generous 1 GB of online storage provided with a standard .Mac account? To add some digital room to your iDisk, you can open the .Mac pane of System Preferences, click the iDisk tab, and then click the Buy More button.

This opens your Web browser and guides you through a three-step upgrade process in which you indicate that you want to buy more iDisk storage, provide payment (the system remembers the credit card you used to subscribe to .Mac), and confirm your purchase.

Your new iDisk capacity should be available within a few minutes of making the purchase.

Figure 3.30 Your iDisk, when mounted, looks and behaves like any other storage device.

Figure 3.31 You can copy files to your iDisk from just about any volume—hard drive, CD, or FireWire hard drive. In this case, we're copying files from a camping-pictures folder on a Mac's hard drive, although the mechanism is the same for any medium.

Moving Files

After you've mounted your iDisk, copying files to it is a breeze. Your iDisk acts like any other disk, so saving files to it and removing files from it is as easy as dragging and dropping. But since you're connected to your iDisk via a network, copying files is likely to be slower than if you were copying them to another hard drive (unless you happen to have a mighty fat, super-low-latency pipe at your home or business).

To copy a file to your iDisk:

1. Mount your iDisk.

   The iDisk is now available for file transfers (**Figure 3.30**).

2. Open a new window, navigate to the files that you want to copy to your iDisk, and select them (**Figure 3.31**).

3. Drag the selected files to the appropriate folder on your iDisk.

   The selected items are copied to your iDisk.

To remove a file from your iDisk:

1. Mount your iDisk (see Figure 3.30).
   The iDisk is now available for file transfers.

2. Open the folder containing the files that you want to delete from your iDisk, and select them (**Figure 3.32**).

3. *Do one of the following:*
   ▲ Drag the selected files to the Trash (**Figure 3.33**).
   ▲ From the Finder's File menu, choose Move to Trash (or press Command-Delete) (**Figure 3.34**).
   A dialog pops up noting that the items will be deleted immediately (**Figure 3.35**).

4. Click OK.
   The files are removed from your iDisk.

Figure 3.32 To delete files and folders from your iDisk, first find and select them.

Figure 3.33 To delete a file from your iDisk, drag it to the Trash.

Figure 3.34 You can also select Move to Trash from the Finder's File menu to delete a file.

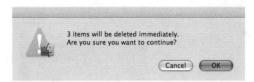

Figure 3.35 When you delete items from your iDisk, a dialog opens, asking for confirmation. Click OK.

Figure 3.36 The main .Mac page prior to when you log in gives all kinds of basic information about .Mac.

Figure 3.37 Type your member name and password in the .Mac login page, and then click Login.

Connecting to Your iDisk with a Browser

Thanks to a .Mac update from January 2006, you can access and download files from your iDisk using nothing but a Web browser and your childlike charm. This is a great alternative for the times when you don't want to mount your iDisk as a network volume. Web browsers are easy to come by, and you might not want to mount the iDisk in Mac OS X or bother with downloading iDisk software for Windows.

To connect to your iDisk with a Web browser, you'll need to use Safari 2.0.2 or later or Firefox 1.0.4 or later (on a Mac), or Internet Explorer 6 or later or Firefox 1.0.4 or later (on Windows).

To connect to iDisk using a Web browser:

1. Using a Web browser, go to www.mac.com.

   The main .Mac page loads (**Figure 3.36**).

2. Click the Log In button in the upper right corner of the page.

   The .Mac login page loads (**Figure 3.37**).

   continues on next page

3. In the "Member name" and Password fields, type your .Mac member name and password, and then click the Login button.

The main .Mac page reloads, only this time you're logged in (**Figure 3.38**).

4. On the left side of the page, click the iDisk link (about halfway down) (**Figure 3.39**).

A login sheet slides down asking for your member name and password again (**Figure 3.40**).

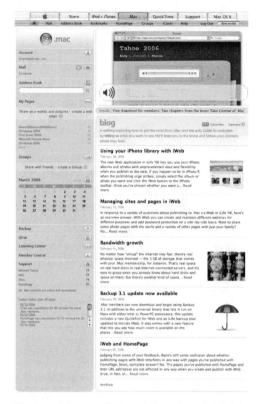

Figure 3.38 Once you've logged in to .Mac, the main .Mac page loads, chock full of useful information.

Figure 3.39 Click the iDisk link on the left side of the page to view your iDisk contents in a browser window.

Figure 3.40 Sometimes—but not always—you will be asked to enter your member name and password again before your iDisk loads in the browser window. (If you've just logged into your iDisk, you won't be asked to verify again.)

Figure 3.41 This Web page looks and works a lot like a Finder window in list mode, and it lists the contents of your iDisk.

5. Enter your .Mac member name and password in the Name and Password fields, and then click Log In (if asked).

Your iDisk page loads, showing all of the files and folders there (**Figure 3.41**).

✔ Tip

- You can view and change your .Mac storage settings at any time by clicking the Storage Settings link in the bottom-right corner of the page.

Using iDisk Utility on a Mac

If you're using a version of Mac OS X that's earlier than Mac OS X v10.3, you should consider downloading and using Apple's iDisk Utility (which you can find on the Member Central download page after you log in to your .Mac account). This gem of a utility lets you password-protect your Public folder and make it accessible to others for uploading. You can also use the utility to see how much space you have left on your iDisk, as well as to open other members' iDisks or Public folders. Although you can use the utility if you're running Mac OS X v10.3 or later, there's no real need to, since all of the features are already built into the OS.

To list a folder's contents on your iDisk using a Web browser:

1. Follow steps 1–5 from "To connect to iDisk using a Web browser."

   Your iDisk page loads, showing all of the files and folders there (see Figure 3.41). This view of your iDisk works like a Finder window in list view, complete with disclosure triangles to the left of folders.

2. Click the disclosure triangle to the left of the folder you want to open.

   The contents of that folder are listed below it (**Figure 3.42**).

3. Click the triangle again.

   The folder returns to its closed state.

✔ Tips

- To return to the root level of your iDisk, click the iDisk Home button at the top of the window.

- You can always see where you are on your iDisk by glancing at the path that appears below the Back/Forward buttons at the top of the page.

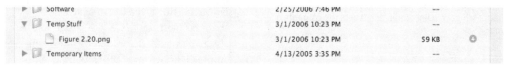

Figure 3.42 A clicked disclosure triangle turns point-downward when its folder's contents are listed; in this case, the contents are just one file.

Figure 3.44 When clicked, the Back button at the top of the page takes you back to the folder you previously opened.

To open a folder on your iDisk using a Web browser:

1. Follow steps 1–5 from "To connect to iDisk using a Web browser."

   Your iDisk page loads, showing all of the files and folders there (see Figure 3.41). This view of your iDisk works like a Finder window in list view.

2. Double-click the folder you want to open.

   The window reloads, listing the folder's contents (**Figure 3.43**).

3. Click the Back button at the top of the page (**Figure 3.44**).

   The window reloads and the original folder's contents are listed—you've just moved back up one level on your iDisk (see Figure 3.44).

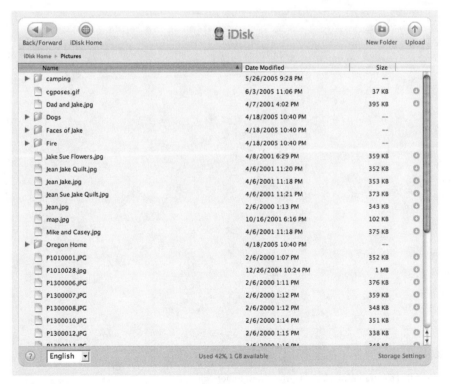

Figure 3.43 After you double-click a folder icon, the contents of that folder are listed in the window—in this case, the contents of the Pictures folder.

To create a folder on your iDisk using a Web browser:

1. Follow steps 1–5 from "To connect to iDisk using a Web browser."

   Your iDisk page loads, showing all of the files and folders there (see Figure 3.41). This view of your iDisk works like a Finder window in list view.

2. Navigate to the location on your iDisk where you want to create the folder (see "To open a folder on your iDisk using a Web browser") (**Figure 3.45**).

   The window loads with the location where you'll be creating a folder.

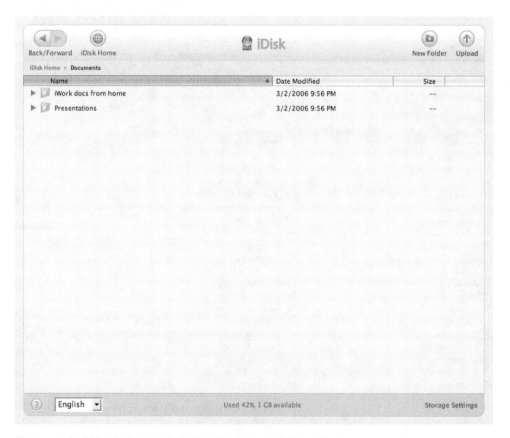

Figure 3.45 The folder that's currently displayed is where new folders will appear.

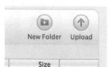

Figure 3.46 Click the New Folder button in the upper-right corner to create a new folder on your iDisk.

Figure 3.47 Type the name of the folder you're creating in the dialog that appears.

Figure 3.48 Type the name of the folder and click OK.

3. Click the New Folder button in the upper right corner of the page (**Figure 3.46**).

A dialog opens, asking for the name of the new folder (**Figure 3.47**).

4. Type the folder's name and click the OK button (**Figure 3.48**).

The new folder appears in your iDisk file and folder list (**Figure 3.49**).

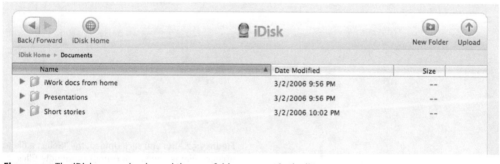

Figure 3.49 The iDisk page reloads, and the new folder appears in the list.

To upload a file to your iDisk using a Web browser:

1. Follow steps 1–5 from "To connect to iDisk using a Web browser."

   Your iDisk page loads, showing all of the files and folders there (see Figure 3.41). This view of your iDisk works like a Finder window in list view.

2. Navigate to the location on your iDisk where you want to upload the file (see "To open a folder on your iDisk using a Web browser") (**Figure 3.50**).

   The window loads with the location where you'll be uploading the file.

3. Click the Upload button in the upper right corner of the page (**Figure 3.51**).

   A dialog opens with the message, "Select a file to upload" (**Figure 3.52**).

Figure 3.50 Uploaded files will be stored in the folder that's currently listed in the browser window.

Figure 3.51 Click the Upload button to begin the process of copying a file to your iDisk.

Figure 3.52 After you click Upload, the "Select a file to upload" dialog appears in your iDisk window. Click Choose File to proceed.

Figure 3.53 Navigate to the folder that contains the file you want to upload.

Figure 3.54 Select the file you want to upload, and click Choose.

Figure 3.55 Once you've selected the file to upload, its name appears in the "Select a file to upload" dialog. Click Upload to copy it to your iDisk.

Figure 3.56 Once uploaded, the file appears in the file list.

4. Click the Choose File button.

A file-selection dialog appears (**Figure 3.53**).

5. In the file-selection dialog, navigate to the file you want to upload and click Choose (**Figure 3.54**).

The filename appears to the right of the Choose File button (**Figure 3.55**).

6. Click the Upload button.

The file is uploaded to your iDisk, and the window reloads, showing the file in the list (**Figure 3.56**).

To download a file from your iDisk using a Web browser:

1. Follow steps 1–5 from "To connect to iDisk using a Web browser."

   Your iDisk page loads, showing all of the files and folders there (see Figure 3.41). This view of your iDisk works like a Finder window in list view.

2. Navigate to the file you want to download (see "To open a folder on your iDisk using a Web browser").

   The window loads, listing the file to be downloaded (**Figure 3.57**).

3. Click the download arrow to the right of the file size (**Figure 3.58**).

   The file downloads to your computer's disk in the location where files are normally downloaded (**Figure 3.59**).

✔ Tip

- When this method is used to download a file that a Web browser can open (such as a JPEG image or HTML file), the file will load in a new browser window instead of downloading to your disk. To actually download the file once it's loaded in the new window, use any method you would normally use to download a file in a window—drag an image to your desktop, or save a movie or sound file using the control in the QuickTime movie player bar.

Figure 3.57 You can download files (but not folders) from the currently loaded iDisk folder.

Figure 3.58 Click the download arrow to the right of the file's size to download the file.

Figure 3.59 The downloaded file appears in the folder where files normally appear when downloaded.

Figure 3.60 Some of your .Mac preferences are built into Mac OS X, and you can click the .Mac icon in the main System Preferences window to access them.

Figure 3.61 The .Mac preference pane defaults to the Account pane, which contains your .Mac member name and password, and it tells you how long you have until you need to resubscribe.

Using the Public Folder

Using your iDisk's Public folder, you can share files and folders with just about anyone who has Internet access. This Public folder is a special folder on your iDisk that others can connect to without having to use your login and password. The settings for controlling it are built into Mac OS X.

Using your System Preferences, you can set access to the Public folder to allow people to see and download files from it, but not upload to it, or to both upload and download files from it. Setting your Public folder to allow people only to download items from it, however, protects you from having someone upload objectionable material or fill up the folder with stuff you don't want or need.

You upload files to this folder as you would any folder on your iDisk. The folder is special, however, in that items inside it can easily be downloaded by anyone who has access to your .Mac member name. If you're sensitive about who can access your iDisk's Public folder, you can give it a password so that only those who know the password can access it.

To set access to your Public folder:

1. From the Apple menu, choose System Preferences.

   The System Preferences window opens.

2. In the Internet & Network section, click the .Mac icon (**Figure 3.60**).

   The .Mac preference pane opens (**Figure 3.61**).

continues on next page

3. Click the iDisk tab.

The iDisk preference pane opens
(**Figure 3.62**).

4. In the Your Public Folder section, *do one of the following:*

▲ To allow users to see and download files from your Public folder but not upload to it, choose the "Read only" radio button.

▲ To allow users to upload and download files to and from your Public folder, choose the "Read & write" radio button.

Your Public folder is ready to be used by others according to the access privileges you've just set.

Figure 3.62 The iDisk preference pane contains good at-a-glance information about your iDisk, including how much storage you have (and have used), whether you have iDisk synchronization turned on, whether you allow others to upload items to your Public folder, and whether that folder is password protected.

Provide Web access to your Public folder

In the spring of 2006, Apple introduced a simplified method for accessing iDisk Public folders, using any Web browser. All the other methods described in this chapter still work, but the easiest way to steer others to your Public folder is to have them aim their browsers at the following URL (typed all on one line, with no spaces): http://idisk.mac.com/membername-Public (replacing "membername" with your .Mac member name). *Note that the "P" in Public must be capitalized for this to work.*

If your Public folder is password-protected, visitors will be prompted for a name and a password. They should enter "public" (without the quotation marks)—not your .Mac member name—in the Name field (which may be filled in for them already). They should type your Public folder password (not, once again, your .Mac account password) in the Password field.

You can use this method to get at your Public folder as well, but if you do, your options will be limited to those you've given the public. If you've made the folder read-only, for example, you won't be able to upload files if you log in this way. For full access to your Public folder contents and settings (and the rest of your iDisk), log in at http://iDisk.mac.com, using your .Mac member name and account password.

Figure 3.63 Check this box to require guests to enter a password before accessing your Public folder.

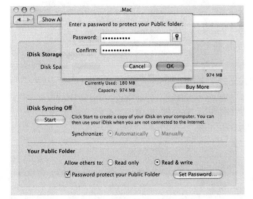

Figure 3.64 Set and confirm a password for your Public folder.

To password-protect your Public folder:

1. Follow Steps 1-3 under "To set access to your Public folder."

2. In the Your Public folder section, check the "Password protect your Public Folder" box (**Figure 3.63**).

   A dialog slides down, asking for password information (**Figure 3.64**).

3. In the Password field, type the password you want to use for your Public folder.

   The text of the password will not appear, but you will see a bullet for each character you type.

4. In the Confirm field, type the password a second time. This ensures that you spelled the password properly.

5. Click OK.

   Your Public folder is password-protected, and you are returned to the iDisk preference pane.

✔ Tips

- Your Public folder password and your .Mac account password cannot be the same. If you need to change your Public folder password, click the Set Password button in the lower right area of the iDisk preference pane.

- Don't give others your .Mac password—this is different from your Public folder password.

USING THE PUBLIC FOLDER

To connect to someone else's Public folder using Mac OS X v10.3 or later:

1. From the Go menu, choose iDisk > Other User's Public Folder (**Figure 3.65**).

   The Connect To iDisk Public Folder dialog opens.

2. In the "Member name" field, enter the .Mac member name for the Public folder to which you're connecting (**Figure 3.66**).

3. If prompted for a password, enter one (**Figure 3.67**).

   The Public folder is mounted on your Desktop, and you can upload and download files to and from it.

Connecting to Someone Else's Public Folder Using Mac OS X v10.2 or Earlier

If you're running an older version of Mac OS X, you can still connect to someone else's iDisk—you'll just have to download and install an Apple-supplied utility to do it.

To connect to a Public folder using Mac OS X v10.2 or earlier, visit the Member Central page (after you log into your .Mac account) and download iDisk Utility. After the download is complete, mount the iDisk Utility disk image by double-clicking it, and then run the installer that you find there.

Once iDisk Utility is installed, run it, and when it opens, click the Open Public Folder button. Enter the member name for the iDisk that you want to connect to, and click Open. The Public folder for the .Mac member you indicated mounts on your Desktop, and you can upload and download files to and from it.

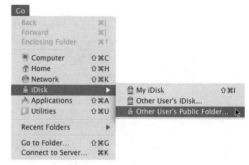

Figure 3.65 To connect to someone else's Public folder, choose Go > iDisk > Other User's Public Folder.

Figure 3.66 Enter the member name of the Public folder to which you want to connect in the Connect To iDisk Public Folder dialog.

Figure 3.67 iDisk shows its WebDAV roots when you connect to a password-protected iDisk. Here, enter the password for the Public folder to which you want to connect (the name "public" is already filled in for you).

USING THE PUBLIC FOLDER

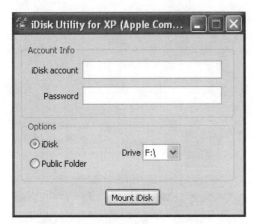

Figure 3.68 iDisk Utility for Windows XP lets you connect to Public folders as well as iDisks.

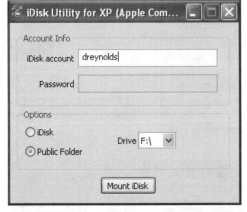

Figure 3.69 Choose the Public Folder radio button, and in the "iDisk account" field type the .Mac member name for the Public folder to which you want to connect.

Figure 3.70 The "Public login" dialog opens if the Public folder has a password.

To connect to someone else's Public folder using Windows XP:

1. Download and install iDisk Utility for Windows as described in steps 1–10 in "To connect to iDisk using Windows XP," earlier in this chapter.

   The iDisk Utility for XP dialog opens (**Figure 3.68**).

2. Choose the Public Folder radio button.

3. In the "iDisk account" field, enter the member name for the Public folder you want to use (**Figure 3.69**).

   If the Public folder has a password, a dialog opens asking you to enter it (**Figure 3.70**). If it doesn't, the iDisk mounts, and a message appears, letting you know that the iDisk has been mounted successfully.

To connect to someone else's Public folder using Windows 2000:

1. Double-click the My Computer icon.

   The My Computer window opens.

2. From the Tools menu, choose Map Network Drive (**Figure 3.71**).

   The Map Network Drive dialog opens.

3. At the bottom of the dialog, click "Create a shortcut to a Web folder or FTP site" (**Figure 3.72**).

   The Add Network Place Wizard dialog opens.

4. In the field marked "Type the location of the Network Place," type http://idisk .mac.com/*membername*-Public? (replacing *membername* with the .Mac member name for the Public folder you're accessing) (**Figure 3.73**).

5. Click Next.

   If the Public folder has a password set, the Enter Network Password dialog opens.

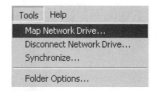

Figure 3.71 To begin creating a connection to a .Mac Public folder in Windows 2000, choose Map Network Drive from the Tools menu.

Figure 3.72 Click "Create a shortcut to a Web folder or FTP site," which will take you to a dialog where you can type in the URL for the Public folder.

Figure 3.73 To connect to a Public folder using Windows 2000, you have to type the URL of the Public folder, and then follow that with -Public?. The URL for my Public folder is shown here as an example.

USING THE PUBLIC FOLDER

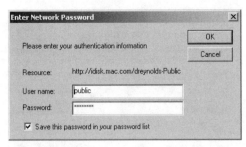

Figure 3.74 Once you've entered a location for the Public folder, you'll be asked for the password—if one is required.

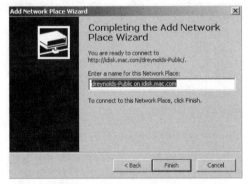

Figure 3.75 When completing the Public folder setup, you'll be asked to name the connection. A suggested name is already entered for you—often, that's descriptive enough for most purposes and you can just click Finish.

Figure 3.76 Once you've finished your Public folder's connection setup, a new window opens, displaying its contents.

6. In the "User name" field, enter `public` (**Figure 3.74**).

7. In the Password field, enter the password for that Public folder.

8. Click OK.

   The Add Network Place Wizard dialog opens, asking you to name your new Network Place.

9. In the Network Place name field, type a name for your Network Place (such as Bill's Public Folder) (**Figure 3.75**).

10. Click Finish.

    The iDisk public folder opens in a new window (**Figure 3.76**).

✔ Tips

■ Having trouble connecting? Make sure the Public folder that you're connecting to has its permissions set properly, or you (or others) may not be able to connect— or will not be able to upload files, at least.

■ A Network Place is a Windows term for a network bookmark—a quick way of connecting to a network service, such as an often-used file server.

About Storage Capacity

Through a built-in control panel, Mac OS X provides an at-a-glance measure of how much space you've used on your iDisk—and how much is available for you to store movies, pictures, Web pages, and other files.

Your .Mac account comes with 1 GB of online storage space, and both your iDisk and .Mac Mail count toward that 1 GB limit. By default, this storage is divided between your iDisk and your e-mail account at 512 MB each, but you have control over how that space is allocated. If you find that either your iDisk or your e-mail account needs more space, you are free to change their storage allotments.

If you're running up against the 1 GB limit, and both your iDisk and e-mail accounts are full, you have two choices: reduce the amount of data you have stored on your .Mac account, or buy more capacity. While conservation is laudable (even storage-space conservation), sometimes the only remedy for cramped quarters is to add some room. You can increase your .Mac storage capacity to 2 GB for $49.95 per year, or 4 GB for $99.95 per year.

To check iDisk usage:

1. From the Apple menu, choose System Preferences.

   The System Preferences window opens.

2. In the Internet & Network section, click the .Mac icon.

   The .Mac preference pane opens.

3. Click the iDisk tab.

   The iDisk preference pane opens. At the top, it displays a gauge that indicates how much iDisk space you've used and how much you have available (**Figure 3.77**). It also attaches numbers to these levels in the form of megabytes currently used and total capacity of your iDisk.

Figure 3.77 The iDisk preference pane is a handy way to see at a glance how much storage you've used.

✔ Tip

■ You can quickly get to the Web page to buy more iDisk storage space by clicking the Buy More button in the iDisk preference pane.

Figure 3.78 To make changes to your iDisk allocation, you must first log in to .Mac using a Web browser. Type your .Mac member name and password in the respective fields.

Figure 3.79 Click the Account link to access your .Mac Account Settings page.

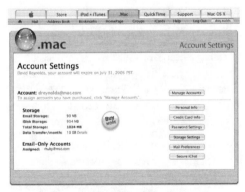

Figure 3.80 Your main .Mac Account Settings page contains entry points to let you change personal information, credit card information, and password settings, and to manage accounts. It also lets you change your iDisk storage allocation.

To reallocate .Mac storage:

1. Go to www.mac.com and log in to your .Mac account (**Figure 3.78**).

2. In the upper left corner of the page, click the Account link (**Figure 3.79**).
   The Account Settings page opens (**Figure 3.80**).

3. Click the Storage Settings button.
   The Storage Settings page opens.

continues on next page

ABOUT STORAGE CAPACITY

4. From the .Mac Mail pop-up menu, choose the amount of storage you want to devote to e-mail (**Figure 3.81**).

The amount allocated to your iDisk will adjust itself according to what you select for your mail to make up the total amount of storage you have available.

5. Click Save.

Your e-mail and iDisk storage allotments automatically reflect the adjusted settings.

✔ Tips

■ Any groups that you've created are assigned a default of 30MB of storage from your iDisk storage pool, split between iDisk and messages. You can adjust this amount by choosing a new amount from the popup menu.

■ The Storage Settings page shows you at a glance how much mail and iDisk storage is being used.

■ The e-mail allocation can never be smaller than 15 MB, and the iDisk allocation can never be smaller than 55 MB.

Figure 3.81 You can allocate new amounts by selecting them from the .Mac Mail pop-up menu. You can also adjust how storage is allocated for any groups that you have created.

Keeping Your Storage Svelte

If you're like most people, you have a lot of junk on your hard drive that you'd never miss if it were to disappear. The same probably goes for your iDisk. While 1 GB is a respectable amount, you can eat that up pretty quickly with movies, music, and pictures—especially if your e-mail account is IMAP-based. Here are some tips for reducing your online storage usage:

◆ **Reduce your mail.** If you're using IMAP, you can save on storage space by getting rid of unwanted messages, especially those with attachments.

◆ **Compress iDisk files.** Use a compression utility to compress files on your iDisk. Mac OS X comes with the Zip archive ability, which is accessible by Control-clicking a file and selecting Create Archive from the contextual menu that pops up.

Figure 3.82 Click Start to turn on iDisk synchronization. This creates a local copy of your iDisk, which you can work with even when you're not connected to the Internet.

Figure 3.83 The local copy of your iDisk sits on your Desktop, just like other volumes.

Creating a Local iDisk Copy

You can set your Mac OS X preferences to make a local copy of your iDisk. This local iDisk is there even if your network is not (such as when you're traveling with your laptop), and it lets you browse the contents of your iDisk very quickly. A local copy of your iDisk takes up space on your hard drive (roughly the same amount as the size of your iDisk), but these days, when 40 GB–plus hard drives occupy the low end of standard equipment, you won't even miss the capacity that a full iDisk copy would take.

If you keep a local copy of your iDisk on your hard drive, you can synchronize it with your "real" iDisk via your Internet connection. To do this, you'll choose from two options: automatic and manual.

To set up your local iDisk in Mac OS X v10.4:

1. From the Apple menu, choose System Preferences.

   The System Preferences window opens.

2. In the Internet & Network section, click the .Mac icon.

   The .Mac preference pane opens.

3. Click the iDisk tab.

   The iDisk preference pane opens.

4. In the iDisk Syncing section, click Start (**Figure 3.82**).

   A local copy of your iDisk is created on your Desktop, and Mac OS X attempts to synchronize the local copy with your online copy by copying files from the remote iDisk to the local iDisk (**Figure 3.83**).

continues on next page

5. *Do one of the following* (**Figure 3.84**):

▲ To set Mac OS X to periodically synchronize your iDisk copy—uploading files you've added, deleting ones you've trashed, or moving ones that you've moved—choose the Synchronize: Automatically radio button.

▲ To set Mac OS X so that it will synchronize your iDisk copy only when you tell it to do so, choose the Synchronize: Manually radio button.

6. Close System Preferences.

Your synchronization process is complete, and your local iDisk copy is ready for use. When the disk is synchronized, newly added items will be uploaded to your Web-based iDisk. The same goes for deleted and moved items—changes are made on your Web-based iDisk when synchronization takes place.

Figure 3.84 When setting up a local copy of your iDisk, you'll need to choose whether or not your iDisk is synchronized automatically.

✔ Tips

■ To manually synchronize your iDisk, click the circular arrow button to the right of the iDisk icon in the sidebar of any Finder window.

■ Change whether your local iDisk is synchronized automatically or manually at any time by opening the iDisk preferences and clicking the appropriate radio button.

■ Setting up a local iDisk in Mac OS X v10.3 is almost the same as setting it up in Mac OS X v10.4, except that instead of starting iDisk Syncing, you simply check a box for "Create a local copy of your iDisk."

CREATING A LOCAL IDISK COPY

USING HOMEPAGE

HomePage is a Web-site tool that lets you create Web pages with files stored on your iDisk. Using any of the templates that come with HomePage, you can whip up a Web site in minutes—without having to know a lick of HTML.

Your .Mac Web pages are great for sharing pictures, movies, or files with friends and family. They're not so great, however, for running a business. For a business site, you'll probably want features that .Mac doesn't offer, such as forums, shopping carts, and customized domains. If that's the case, you'll need to host your site through a company that specializes in Web hosting. And remember—since your iDisk is where you post your Web pages (and accompanying media), your site is limited by the amount of space on your iDisk.

Most users, however, will find that HomePage makes up for its lack of business features through ease of use and a slew of professional-looking templates. You can use HomePage to create your Web pages—which is perfect if you don't know HTML or just don't have the time to create a custom site—or you can create your site in any other Web authoring tool and host the pages on your .Mac account. I'll cover both options in this chapter.

Creating a Web Page

Can you really create a Web page in a matter of minutes? You betcha. Although the templates and reasons for creating a Web page may vary, the process remains largely the same, no matter what type of page you create. And that's the great thing about your .Mac account—it provides a bunch of templates and does all the dirty work for you; all you need to do is provide the pictures or movies you want to show off, and write some text describing what you're publishing.

It goes something like this: When publishing a page using .Mac and HomePage, you log in to the HomePage section of the .Mac Web site; select a template to use as a starting point for your page; connect pictures, movies, or files on your iDisk to the template; write some text for your page; and publish it.

Don't worry—I'll go over these steps in detail. Publishing a Web page with HomePage isn't a long process—with a little practice, you can put a photo album on the Web in 10 minutes or less.

I'll describe how to upload files such as pictures and movies for your Web pages, which templates are available, and how to create Web pages using the HomePage tool.

HomePage versus iWeb

While it's not an eternal question along the lines of paper or plastic, one thing you should grapple with early is, "Should I use HomePage or iWeb?" Don't worry—we'll cover both.

HomePage is built into .Mac, it's super-easy to use, and you're able to work with it using a Web browser. It walks you through the creation process in a step-by-step fashion, so use HomePage if you're new to publishing pages (or if you don't have iLife '06).

iWeb is a stand-alone application that you can use to build just about any Web page you like. While iWeb's templates make it easy to get started, the application is a good deal more powerful and flexible than HomePage. Use iWeb if you want to diverge from the HomePage templates and feel more confident about creating your own pages. One thing to note—although iWeb will give you more freedom, it still won't give you business-site features, such as a shopping cart or purchase processing. For those, you'll have to find a good Web hosting company.

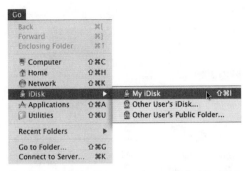

Figure 4.1 From the Go menu, choose iDisk > My iDisk to connect to your iDisk.

Figure 4.2 Enter your .Mac member name and password in the Connect To iDisk dialog, and then click Connect to connect to your iDisk.

Figure 4.3 Once mounted, your iDisk works like any other network volume.

Uploading Files

Although I covered how to copy files to your iDisk in Chapter 3, it's central enough to using HomePage that we'll cover the basics again here. For complete information on iDisk, including connecting to iDisk and uploading files, see Chapter 3, "Using iDisk."

The reason iDisk is so important when publishing a Web page using .Mac is that Home-Page looks to iDisk for the pictures, movies, and other files that it displays on each Web page. If a file is not on your iDisk, you can't publish it on the Web with HomePage.

To upload a file to your iDisk:

1. From the Go menu, choose iDisk > My iDisk (Command-Shift-I) (**Figure 4.1**).

   The Connect To iDisk dialog opens, asking for your .Mac member name and password (unless you've already entered that information in System Preferences, in which case your iDisk mounts automatically on your Desktop).

2. Enter your .Mac member name and password, and click Connect (**Figure 4.2**).

   Your iDisk mounts on your Desktop, and you can use it like any other volume (**Figure 4.3**). The connection to your iDisk is maintained until you disconnect it or shut down your computer.

   continues on next page

3. Open a new Finder window, navigate to the files you want to copy to your iDisk, and select them (**Figure 4.4**).

4. Drag the selected files to the appropriate folder on your iDisk (**Figure 4.5**).

The selected items are successfully copied to your iDisk.

✔ Tip

■ Remember—image files must be placed inside the Pictures folder on your iDisk (or a subfolder of Pictures) in order for HomePage to find them. Same goes for movie files.

Figure 4.4 Before you copy files to the iDisk, you need to navigate to them.

Figure 4.5 To copy files to your iDisk, drag them to the folder to which you want to copy them.

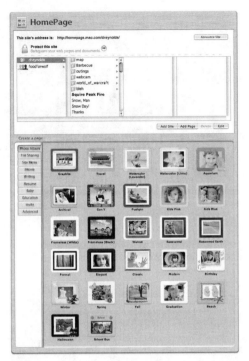

Figure 4.6 When you first load the HomePage section of the .Mac members' Web site, you're presented with its main interface. The top portion lists all of your sites and pages within those sites in column view. The bottom portion shows the templates you can use to quickly create new pages.

About Templates

HomePage comes with hundreds of templates you can use to build your Web pages. These templates are essentially prebuilt Web pages into which you plug your pictures, movies, and text. Although you can build Web pages from scratch and publish them on a .Mac site, .Mac templates spare you all that work and free you from having to know any HTML. You supply the content and HomePage provides the rest: Its main interface lists the kinds of pages you can create, displays thumbnail images of the various templates, and provides a map of the sites and pages published on your .Mac account (**Figure 4.6**).

continues on next page

HomePage templates are divided into the following ten categories (the categories and templates on .Mac sometimes change, so this may not be a complete—or accurate—list):

◆ **Photo Album.** This option provides more than two dozen templates for sharing pictures you've uploaded to the Pictures folder on your iDisk (**Figure 4.7**).

◆ **File Sharing.** These templates help you to create a page that lets visitors download files from your Movies, Pictures, Public, Sites, and Music folders (**Figure 4.8**).

◆ **Site Menu.** Sort of the uber-template, the Site Menu template lets you create a menu page that can be used to navigate the rest of your .Mac site (**Figure 4.9**).

Figure 4.7 The extensive Photo Album template set is a quick way to get your digital albums online.

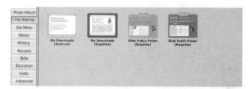

Figure 4.8 The File Sharing template set makes it easy to create a page allowing others to download files from your .Mac Web site (including your Public folder).

Figure 4.9 The Site Menu template set allows you to pull together an index page that points to several other Web pages—either within your .Mac Web site or on external sites.

Figure 4.10 The iMovie template set lets you easily put your movies online.

Figure 4.11 The Writing template set provides some attractive starting points for text-based pages, such as newsletters.

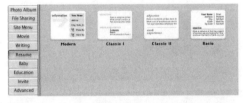

Figure 4.12 The Resume template set makes it easy for you to post your résumé online for others to read.

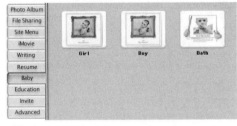

Figure 4.13 The Baby template set helps you get the word out about that new addition.

♦ **iMovie.** More than a dozen templates in this category let you showcase movies you upload to your iDisk Movies folder (**Figure 4.10**).

♦ **Writing.** Well, we've already seen templates for sharing pictures, movies, and files, so why not some for text? Choose from more than a dozen templates for creating text-based Web pages. Some of these pages feature images from your iDisk Pictures folder, but no files are needed to add text; all you have to do is type your prose into some HomePage text fields (**Figure 4.11**).

♦ **Resume.** Looking for a job? Might be worth filling out these templates to tempt potential employers. You essentially fill in the blanks; you won't need to upload files to your iDisk (**Figure 4.12**).

♦ **Baby.** As of this writing, HomePage offers three templates for creating baby announcements: Girl, Boy, and Bath (**Figure 4.13**).

continues on next page

◆ **Education.** Tailored to schools and educators, these templates include designs pertaining to school events, sports teams, school news, homework, and more (**Figure 4.14**).

◆ **Invite.** Throwing a party? Choose from templates that include Birthday, Football, and Picnic themes (**Figure 4.15**).

◆ **Advanced.** This option lets you publish files you've created using an HTML editor or other external Web authoring tool (**Figure 4.16**). Not technically a template (you can't plug content into it—you build the page yourself from the ground up), it's included in the template list for simplicity's sake.

Figure 4.14 The Education template set gives those involved in education (such as teachers and coaches) specialized pages.

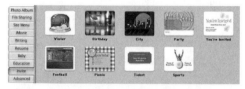

Figure 4.15 The Invite template set is an easy way to put up an electronic invitation to a party, sporting event, or other gathering.

Figure 4.16 One lonely item in the Advanced section allows you to integrate any HTML page into your .Mac site.

Figure 4.17 The first step in creating a photo album is to upload the pictures you want to put in that album to your iDisk's Pictures folder.

Figure 4.18 Type your .Mac member name and password into the fields on the .Mac login page, and click the Login button to log in to the .Mac members' section.

Creating a Photo Album

The most popular type of .Mac Web page has got to be the photo album. E-mailing digital photos to friends and family members can feel like a chore, especially once you realize how easy it is to post your pictures to the Web using one of HomePage's Photo Album templates. Each Photo Album template displays a set of photos you publish as thumbnail images that, when clicked, expand to reveal full-size images. HomePage generates the thumbnails automatically, so you don't have to worry about resizing your images. Published Photo Album pages also give visitors the option of viewing all their images in a slide show, at full size. Photo Album pages are perfect for sharing digital photos of special events and are practically mandatory for new parents.

To create a .Mac photo album:

1. Upload the photos you want to use in your photo album to your iDisk's Pictures folder (**Figure 4.17**). Place the photos you want to appear together in the album inside their own folder within the Pictures folder. If you plan on making more than one album page, place the files for each page in a separate folder—for example, birthday1, birthday2, and so on.

2. Using a Web browser, go to www.mac.com and log in to your .Mac account (**Figure 4.18**).

   The main .Mac members' page loads.

   continues on next page

3. Click the HomePage link at the top (**Figure 4.19**).

The main HomePage page loads (**Figure 4.20**). By default, it opens to the Photo Album page.

4. If the Photo Album tab is not already selected, click it to select it (**Figure 4.21**).

The Photo Album templates are displayed.

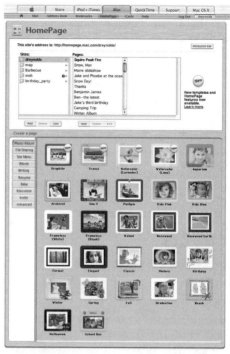

Figure 4.20 The main HomePage page defaults automatically to the Photo Album page.

Figure 4.19 Click the HomePage link at the top of the page or the link in the left sidebar to load the HomePage tool.

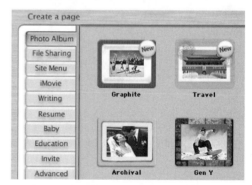

Figure 4.21 If it's not selected for some reason, click the Photo Album tab to load the Photo Album templates, and then click the thumbnail of the template you want to use.

Figure 4.22 To choose photos for your photo album, click the folder that contains the photos you want to use in the "Choose a folder" window. Once done, click Choose.

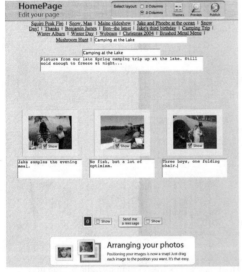

Figure 4.23 In the "Edit your page" page, fill in the fields in the chosen photo album template to complete the page. Here, you'll have to fill in a page title, a page description, and brief descriptions for each picture.

5. Select the template you want to use to display your photos from the ones on the Photo Album page.

   The "Choose a folder" page loads, displaying the contents of your iDisk's Pictures folder (**Figure 4.22**). Take the name of this page literally. Photos must be saved to a folder within your Pictures folder on your iDisk to be uploaded as a group.

6. Click the folder that houses the pictures you want to use in the photo album, and then click Choose.

   The "Edit your page" page loads (**Figure 4.23**).

7. *Fill in the following fields:*

   ▲ In the field at the top of the page, type a name for your Web page. This will appear in the index at the top of your main .Mac homepage.

   ▲ In the page title field, type a title for the page itself.

   ▲ In the text box below the title field, type a few sentences explaining what your page is about.

   ▲ In the text box below each picture, type a label or caption.

8. If you want your album to contain a "hit counter" that tracks visits to the page, check the Show box to the right of the number 0 at the bottom of the page.

continues on next page

9. If you want to include a "Send me a message" button (which viewers can click to send you an e-mail message), check the Show box to the right of the "Send me a message" button.

10. In the "Select layout" section in the upper right corner of the page, *do one of the following:*

▲ Click the 2 Columns radio button to display your photos in a set of two columns on the page (**Figure 4.24**).

▲ Click the 3 Columns radio button to display your photos in a set of three columns on the page (**Figure 4.25**).

The page refreshes to display your new layout.

Figure 4.24 Click the 2 Columns radio button to choose the two-column layout for your photo album.

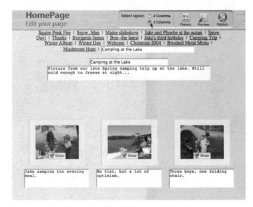

Figure 4.25 Click the 3 Columns radio button to choose the three-column layout for your photo album.

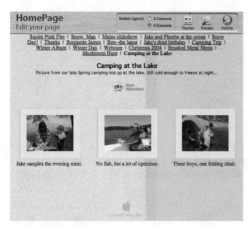

Figure 4.26 To preview your page, click the Preview button.

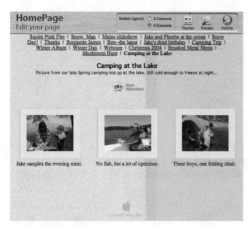

Figure 4.27 The final step in publishing your site is the Congratulations page, which gives you the URL for your new page as well as the opportunity to send an iCard announcing the page.

11. If you want to see what your page will look like before publishing it, click the Preview button at the top of the page (**Figure 4.26**).

The page refreshes, displaying a preview of your page.

12. If you did not choose to preview your page, *do one of the following:*

▲ If you're satisfied with how things look, click the Publish button at the top of the page.

▲ If you want to make changes to your page, click Edit to go back and make changes before publishing your page (the edit button only appears when you're previewing a page).

After you've clicked the Publish button, you're presented with the site's URL, and the opportunity to send an iCard to friends and family announcing the site (**Figure 4.27**).

✔ Tips

■ To prevent a photo from showing up on your Web page, uncheck its Show box.

■ To arrange the pictures in a different order than the one shown, simply drag them to their new locations.

Creating a Movie Page

Thanks to broadband Internet access (for some of us lucky souls, at least), we can easily view movies online. (And if you don't have broadband Internet access, you probably shouldn't be uploading video to .Mac.) Thanks to your .Mac account, you can upload your own movies for others to view. Creating a movie page follows the same basic process as creating a photo album.

To create a movie page:

1. Upload the movie you want to share to your iDisk's Movies folder.

2. Go to www.mac.com using a Web browser, and log in to your .Mac account (**Figure 4.28**).

   The main .Mac members' page loads.

3. Click the HomePage link.

   The main HomePage page loads.

4. On the lower left side of the page, click the iMovie tab.

   The iMovie templates load (**Figure 4.29**).

Figure 4.28 Enter your .Mac member name and password in the appropriate fields on the login page.

Figure 4.29 The iMovie templates page lets you choose from a number of templates for your uploaded iMovie, including seasonal templates as well as event-based templates.

Figure 4.30 On the "Edit your page" page, you set up the specifics of your new iMovie page.

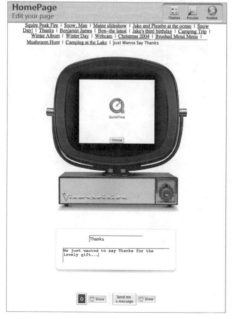

Figure 4.31 To complete the iMovie page, give it a name and a brief description of the page.

5. Click the template you want to use (my fave is Retro-TV).

The "Edit your page" page loads (**Figure 4.30**).

6. *Fill in the following fields* (**Figure 4.31**):

▲ In the field at the top of the page, type a name for your Web page, which will serve as the page's link and appear in the index at the top of your main .Mac homepage.

▲ Type a name for your movie.

▲ Type a brief description of what your movie is about.

continues on next page

7. If you want a hit counter, check the Show box to the right of the number 0 at the bottom of the page (**Figure 4.32**).

8. If you want to include a "Send me a message" button, check the Show box to the right of the "Send me a message" button, as shown in Figure 4.32.

9. Just below the QuickTime logo, click the Choose button as shown in Figure 4.32.

The "Choose a file" page opens (**Figure 4.33**).

Figure 4.32 To have a hit counter included on your Web page, check the Show box to the right of the number 0 at the bottom of the page.

Figure 4.33 Select the movie you want to use on your iMovie page, and then click Choose.

Figure 4.34 After you've selected the movie you want to include on your new page and clicked Preview, the page reloads, appearing as others will see it.

Figure 4.35 Click the Edit button to make changes to your movie page, or click Publish to post it.

Figure 4.36 When you've published your iMovie page, the page's URL is shown, and you're given the opportunity to send an iCard announcing it.

10. Click a movie to select it, and then click Choose.

You're returned to the "Edit your page" page.

11. At the top of the page, click Preview.

The page displaying your movie loads (**Figure 4.34**).

12. If you need to make changes, click the Edit button at the top of the page (**Figure 4.35**).

or

If you're satisfied with how it looks, click Publish.

A Congratulations page loads, containing the movie page's URL and giving you the opportunity to send an iCard announcing the new page (**Figure 4.36**).

✔ Tips

■ Although the tab says iMovie, don't worry—you can create your video using a different video-editing package and still use it here, as long as QuickTime understands it. For example, the AVI movies that many still cameras take work just fine.

■ You can also select a movie from your Pictures, Public, or Sites folder.

CREATING A MOVIE PAGE

Creating a File-Download Page

If you want to provide an easy way for people to download files from your iDisk's Public folder, you're in luck: HomePage includes a few file-download templates.

To create a file-download page:

1. Upload the files you want to share to your iDisk's Public folder.

2. Using a Web browser, go to www.mac.com and log in to your .Mac account.

   The main .Mac members' page loads.

3. Click the HomePage link.

   The main HomePage page loads.

4. On the lower left side of the page, click the File Sharing tab.

   The File Sharing templates load (**Figure 4.37**). There are two types of templates here: My Downloads templates and iDisk Public Folder templates. The My Downloads templates allow you to offer downloads of specific files, anywhere on your iDisk; the iDisk Public Folder templates list the files in your iDisk's Public folder.

5. Click the File Sharing template that you want to use.

   The "Edit your page" page loads for the selected template. What you do next depends on whether you chose a My Downloads template or an iDisk Public Folder template.

6. If you chose a My Downloads template, *do the following* (**Figure 4.38**):

   ▲ In the field at the top of the page, type a name for your Web page, which will serve as the page's link and appear at the top of your central .Mac homepage.

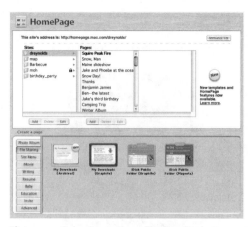

Figure 4.37 To begin creating a file-download page, click the File Sharing template that you want to use.

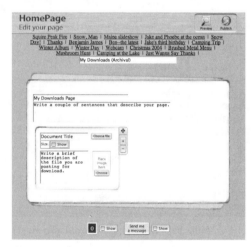

Figure 4.38 If you've chosen a My Downloads template, enter a page title and a brief description, choose an image, and choose a file to be downloaded.

Figure 4.39 If you've chosen an iDisk Public Folder template, enter a page title and a brief description for your page.

▲ Type a few sentences that describe your page. This text will appear below the page's title at the top of your Web page.

▲ In the document title field, type a title for the first file that you're making available as a download.

▲ If you want the file's size to be displayed on the page, check the Show box to the right of the word Size.

▲ In the description text box, write a brief description of the file.

▲ To choose an image for the downloadable file's thumbnail from your iDisk, click the Choose button.

▲ Click the "Choose file" button and navigate to the file you'll be offering for download from your iDisk's Movies, Pictures, Public, Sites, or Music folder.

▲ To add files to a My Downloads page, click the plus (+) button to the right of the file-description area and repeat these steps for the new file. If you have multiple file-description areas on a download page, you can rearrange them by dragging them around by the crossed vertical-and-horizontal-arrow handles in their upper-right corners.

7. If you chose an iDisk Public Folder template, *do the following* (**Figure 4.39**):

▲ In the first field at the top of the page, type a name for your Web page, which will serve as the page's link and appear at the top of your central .Mac homepage.

▲ In the description field, type a description of the contents of your folder.

continues on next page

CREATING A FILE-DOWNLOAD PAGE

8. If you want a hit counter, check the Show box to the right of the number 0 at the bottom of the page.

9. If you want to include a "Send me a message" button (which viewers can use to send you an e-mail message), check the Show box to the right of the "Send me a message" button.

10. To see what the page will look like before you publish it, click Preview.

A preview of the page loads (**Figure 4.40**).

11. If you need to make changes, click Edit. If you're satisfied with how it looks, click Publish.

A Congratulations page loads, displaying the download page's URL and giving you the opportunity to send an iCard announcing the new page (**Figure 4.41**).

✔ Tips

■ If files that you know are in your Public folder aren't appearing in your Public Folder Web-page list, click the Refresh button to see if you can make them appear.

■ To make sure that everyone—regardless of operating system—can work with your files, use care when naming your files. If you stick to uppercase letters, lowercase letters, numbers, hyphens, and under-score characters only (this means no spaces), you ought to be fine. And don't delete filename extensions (such as .jpg or .doc).

■ My Downloads templates let you specify files from any folder on your iDisk, so they don't require you to place download files in the Public folder.

■ To remove a file from a My Downloads page, click the minus (–) button to the right of its description area.

Figure 4.40 After you click the Preview button, the page loads as others would see it—giving you the opportunity to make any needed last-minute changes.

Figure 4.41 When you've published your File Sharing page, you're given the page's URL and the opportunity to send an iCard announcing it.

Figure 4.42 To edit a page, select it in the proper column and then click the Edit button below the Pages column.

Editing Pages

Spelling being what it is, sometimes, you may need to make changes to a .Mac Web page or perhaps delete a page you no longer need. You can change anything about your Web pages—template colors, layout options, captions, you name it—quickly and easily.

To edit an existing page:

1. Log in to your .Mac account using a Web browser, and click the HomePage link.

   The main HomePage page loads.

2. At the top of the page, select the page you want to edit, and click the Edit button (**Figure 4.42**).

   The "Edit your page" page loads, displaying your page in its editable form.

Say It with an iCard

After you create a new .Mac Web page, the first thing you'll want to do is tell people about it. Thanks to iCards, that's a breeze. When you finish creating a new site, a page opens asking if you want to send an iCard announcement. Click the arrow button at the bottom of the page, and you're taken to a special iCard template page, where crafting a quick card with your URL is as easy as filling in the blanks (**Figure 4.43**).

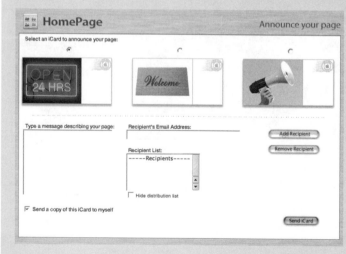

Figure 4.43 To send an iCard announcing your new page, simply choose a template, type a message, and add e-mail addresses to which you'll be sending it. When finished, click Send iCard.

To delete an existing page:

1. Log in to your .Mac account using a Web browser, and click the HomePage link.

   The main HomePage page loads.

2. At the top of the page, select the page you want to delete, and click the Delete button (**Figure 4.44**).

   A warning appears, noting that deleting a page is permanent and asking if you want to continue.

3. Click Yes.

   Your Web page is deleted.

Figure 4.44 To delete a page, select it in the proper column and then click the Delete button.

Figure 4.45 To add a new site, click the Add Site button.

Figure 4.46 Give the site a name on the "Create a site" page. Check the Password: On box, and type in a password to protect the site.

Figure 4.47 Your new site appears as a folder in the second column from the left. Above, a URL for the page is displayed. Of course, no pages are on the site yet—you'll have to add those.

Creating a Site

When you've created a series of Web pages that you'd like to tie together into a logical group, you may be best served by creating a site. This groups a set of pages together for easier access. Your .Mac account not only makes it easy to create a Web page, but it also lets you manage multiple Web sites with the same set of tools.

To create a site:

1. Log in to your .Mac account using a Web browser, and click the HomePage link.

   The main HomePage page loads.

2. On the right side of the page below the columns, click the Add Site button (**Figure 4.45**).

   The "Create a site" page loads.

3. In the Site Name field, type the name for your site.

4. If you want to password-protect your site, check the Password: On box.

5. If you've checked the Password: On box, type your password in the Password field (**Figure 4.46**).

6. Click the Create Site button.

   The main HomePage page loads, with a note at the top indicating the URL of the newly created site. A folder (with the site's name to the right) appears in the second column (**Figure 4.47**).

✔ Tips

- You can't use spaces in your site names.

- .Mac site names are case-sensitive.

- Don't use your .Mac password for a site's password. If you do, the people to whom you give the site's address and password will also have the keys to your .Mac account.

dd a page to a site:

1. Log in to your .Mac account using a Web browser, and click the HomePage link. The main HomePage page loads.

2. In the second column, click the folder of the site to which you want to add a new page (see Figure 4.47).

3. Click the Add Page button (**Figure 4.48**). The "Select a theme" page opens. From here, you can create any type of page you like, as described earlier in this chapter.

✔ Tip

- You can move a page from one site to another by dragging the page you want to move to the new site folder in the main HomePage interface.

Figure 4.48 To add a new page to a site, first click the site's folder in the second column from the left, and then click the Add Page button.

Getting to Your New Web Site

Once you've created a Web site, others can see it at the following address:

http://homepage.mac.com/*membername*/

Of course, be sure to replace *member-name* with your .Mac member name. This will take folks to your main .Mac home-page. To specify a different site published to your .Mac account, use this URL:

http://homepage.mac.com/*membername*/*sitename*/

In the URL above, replace *membername* with your .Mac member name and *site-name* with the site name that you specify. This takes people to the specified site in *sitename*.

You can always find a site's URL by log-ging in to HomePage and selecting the site (on the left). The URL will appear at the top of the page in blue (see Figure 4.49).

Figure 4.49 The first step in creating a site menu is to select the site in the second column from the left and then click the Site Menu tab to load the Site Menu template set.

Figure 4.50 To create a site menu, fill in a title for the page, and a title and description for each item on the page.

Creating a Site Menu

Now that you've created all these great Web pages, it's time to organize them with a site menu—and for that, we'll need the Site Menu template. A site menu provides visitors with a high-level overview of the pages in a site that you've created using your .Mac account. The site menu should be one of the last things you do when creating a site—it ties all those pages into a coherent whole.

To create a site menu:

1. Log in to your .Mac account using a Web browser, and click the HomePage link.

   The main HomePage page loads.

2. In the second column from the left, at the top of the page, select the site for which you want to create a site menu, and then click the Site Menu tab (**Figure 4.49**).

   The Site Menu templates load.

3. Click a Site Menu template.

   The "Edit your page" page loads for that selected template. This page shows all of the site's individual Web pages.

4. Fill in all of the text fields, writing a title and description for the page, and a title and description for each item (**Figure 4.50**).

continues on next page

5. To choose a picture to represent each page accessible from the site menu, click the Choose button within each image and select a picture in the "Choose a file" page (**Figure 4.51**).

You can use appropriate photos from your own Pictures folder or make a selection from the HomePage Image Library—a collection of artwork you can plunder for your own purposes. This selection of high-class clip art is organized by category, so it's easy to find something you might like. To do so, simply navigate to the Image Library rather than the Pictures folder (**Figure 4.52**).

6. To remove a page from the site menu you are creating, click the minus (–) button next to each page you want removed from the site menu (**Figure 4.53**).

The page reloads sans the items you clicked.

Figure 4.52 If you don't have a photo of your own to match a Site Menu entry, you can probably find one that works in the HomePage Image Library.

Figure 4.53 To remove an item from a site-menu page, click the minus (–) button in its upper right corner.

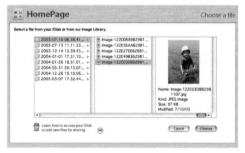

Figure 4.51 Click the picture you want to use as the representative graphic for the site menu item, and then click Choose to set the image.

Figure 4.54 To add a new item linking to another page (or to an e-mail address), click the plus (+) button in the upper right corner of the item you want to have appear *before* the new item.

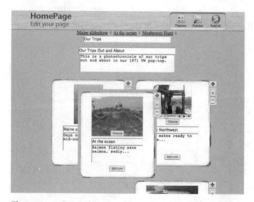

Figure 4.55 Repositioning items on a site-menu page is as easy as dragging the upper right corner of the item until the item is where you want it to be—place it between two items to have the moved item appear between them.

7. To add a new page (or external link) to the site menu you are creating, click the plus (+) button next to the item that comes before the place where you want to add a new item (**Figure 4.54**).

   The page reloads with a new item. See the sidebar "Adding Links to Your Site Menu" for details on how to do this.

8. To reposition any item on the site-menu page, drag the crossed-arrows icon on its right side to move it (**Figure 4.55**).

9. To preview your site menu before publishing it, click the Preview button.

10. If you're satisfied, click the Publish button.

    Your site-menu page is published, and the Congratulations page loads with the URL to your new page.

11. If you want the site menu to be the first page visitors see when they visit the site, drag its page icon to the topmost spot in the site's page list on the HomePage page. Its name will appear in boldface, indicating that it's the default page for the site.

Adding Links to Your Site Menu

Remember that plus (+) button next to each item on the Site Menu template (see Figure 4.55)? That button lets you link to the following items from your site menu:

◆ Another page from your .Mac account

◆ An external Web page

◆ An e-mail address

To create a section that links to any of these items from your site menu, click the plus button next to the Web page to which you want to add the link. Don't worry, you won't remove the existing page—the section for adding the link appears after it. Customize this one as you would any other section within a site-menu page by typing a title and description and choosing a graphic element (**Figure 4.56**).

To create the new link, click the Edit Link button. The "Edit your links" page opens. Select from the My Pages, Other Pages, and Email tabs (**Figure 4.57**). Here's what each one does:

◆ **My Pages.** This pane lets you link only to pages that you've created through your .Mac account. In the My Pages pane, select a page to link to it from the site menu, and click Apply.

◆ **Other Pages.** This pane lets you link to pages other than the ones you've created yourself through your .Mac account. In the Other Pages pane, type into the field the URL of the page you want to link to from the site menu, and click Apply.

◆ **Email.** This pane lets you link an item on your Web page to an e-mail address. In the Email pane, type into the field the e-mail address that you'd like to link to, and click Apply.

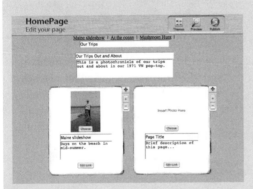

Figure 4.56 A new item on a site-menu page is mostly blank—it's up to you to select a graphic and type in a page title and description.

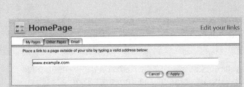

Figure 4.57 By clicking the Edit Link button on an item in a site menu, you can link to another .Mac element, a Web page outside of .Mac, or an e-mail address.

Figure 4.58 To edit a site, click its name in the second column from the left, and then click the Edit button.

Figure 4.59 When the "Edit your site" page loads, you can change the site's name and either assign or remove a password.

Editing Sites

Web sites are not set in stone. After you've created your site, you're likely to want to go back occasionally and change it. Although you'll make most of your changes to individual pages, which we've already covered in this chapter, you can make a few site-wide changes, should the need arise. You can change the name of the site, change the password, or delete the site altogether.

To edit a site:

1. Log in to your .Mac account using a Web browser, and click the HomePage button.
   The main HomePage page loads.

2. In the second column from the left, select the site that you want to edit (**Figure 4.58**).

3. Click the Edit button.
   The "Edit your site" page loads.

4. *Do one or all of the following* (**Figure 4.59**):
   ▲ In the Site Name field, type in a new name for your site.

   ▲ If you'd like to set a password for the site, check the Password: On box, if it isn't already checked, and type a password in the field below it.

   ▲ If you'd like to remove password protection from your site, uncheck the Password: On box.

   ▲ If you'd like to change the password for your site, type in a new password.

5. Click Apply Changes.
   Your new site settings are applied automatically.

EDITING SITES

To delete a site:

1. Log in to your .Mac account using a Web browser, and click the HomePage button. The main HomePage page loads.

2. In the second column from the left select the site that you want to delete.

3. Click the Delete button. The "Delete your site" page loads, asking if you're sure you want to delete the site.

4. Click Yes. Your site is deleted.

✔ Tip

■ To reorder the pages within a site, drag them up or down in the list on the main HomePage page. The top page in the list for a given site is the one that loads first when the site is visited—it becomes the index for that site.

Forwarding a Domain Name to Your .Mac Site

If you've spent the $10 or so to register your own domain name, you can use your registrar's domain-redirect function to redirect people to your .Mac site instead. Here's how it works. If people type in

http://www.*yourfancydomain*.com

they're sent to

http://homepage.mac.com/*membername*/index.html.

This process varies a bit from registrar to registrar, but the essential thing to note is that you're simply forwarding your domain to your .Mac site. If you remember that, making changes with your registrar ought to be easy.

Advanced Web Publishing

Although your .Mac account isn't a full-service professional-level Web hosting account, it is capable of doing more than publishing photo albums and file-download pages. In fact, as long as your Web pages don't rely on fancy services such as CGIs, PHP scripts, or databases, then the sky is the limit (or, at least your proficiency with an HTML authoring application is the limit).

Custom .Mac Web pages can be set up to look and feel just about any way you like, and you can host movies and pictures, publish blogs—anything you can do with HTML and static files that you upload to your iDisk.

So, if Apple's templates just aren't doing it for you, it's OK to code your own. A great crash course in HTML Web design is Elizabeth Castro's *Creating a Web Page with HTML: Visual QuickProject Guide* (Peachpit Press, 2004). She also wrote the best-selling *HTML for the World Wide Web with XHTML and CSS: Visual QuickStart Guide, 6th Edition* (Peachpit Press, 2006).

In this section of this book, you'll learn how to integrate a custom-coded Web page into your .Mac account's main page.

Integrating a Custom Site

If you're here, you've taken the time to learn HTML or a graphical Web-page editor, and you've created a fabulous site that blows away the already-great templates provided by Apple. Now, it's time to take the plunge and put your site up for everyone else to browse.

With .Mac, there are two ways to do this: You can integrate custom-built pages into an existing site created in HomePage, or you can publish one or more pages as a site that stands on its own, separate from the HomePage organizing scheme. The standalone option is described in the "Publishing a Custom Site Sans HomePage" sidebar; we'll look at the HomePage-integration option here.

The benefit of publishing a custom page this way is that the page appears in the list of links in your .Mac site menu (and optionally includes a page-visit counter and contact link). The drawback is that you sacrifice some ability to organize page content exactly as you might like, and the page is surrounded by the .Mac interface, which may not be an ideal complement to your design.

To integrate a custom site:

1. Gather the HTML files that you'll publish on your .Mac site, along with any supporting files (such as images, Flash animations, or movies), and put them in a folder.

2. Connect to your iDisk, and upload the contents of your site's folder (not the folder itself) to your iDisk's Sites folder. If you upload the whole folder, you can still connect to the site, but you won't be able to use the External HTML template to integrate it into your site (**Figure 4.60**).

Figure 4.60 Drag a custom HTML file to your iDisk's Sites folder to upload that file in preparation for integration into your .Mac site.

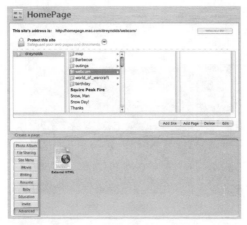

Figure 4.61 The Advanced template tab lists just one item—External HTML. This lets you connect any HTML file you create to your .Mac site.

Figure 4.62 When you load External HTML, you are asked to locate the HTML document you uploaded. Click it, and then click Choose.

3. Log in to your .Mac account using a Web browser, and click the HomePage link.

The main HomePage page loads.

4. At the bottom of the list of tabs, click the Advanced tab (**Figure 4.61**).

The Advanced templates page loads, showing one template: External HTML.

5. Click the External HTML template button.

The "Choose your web page" page loads. The HTML file that you uploaded in step 2 should show up in the Sites folder.

6. Select the HTML file and click Choose (**Figure 4.62**).

The page loads in HomePage on the "Edit your page" page, showing you a preview of how it will look when published.

continues on next page

7. In the title field, type a title for your uploaded page (**Figure 4.63**).

8. If you want a counter or a Send Me a Message link, check the boxes next to these items at the bottom of the page.

9. Click Preview.

A preview of the page loads (**Figure 4.64**).

10. If you need to make changes, click Edit. If you're satisfied with how it looks, click Publish.

A Congratulations page loads with the custom page's URL and gives you the opportunity to send an iCard announcing the new page (**Figure 4.65**).

Once the custom Web site is uploaded, you can connect to it without doing anything else. Simply point your browser to http://homepage.mac.com/*membername*/*filename*, where *membername* is your .Mac member name, and *filename* is the name of the page you've just uploaded.

✔ Tips

■ As long as your links all point to the proper places, you can host a whole Web site, with as many pages, graphics, and supporting files as your iDisk capacity will allow.

■ To publish a custom HTML page to a site other than the default site, first create the site using HomePage, and then upload the HTML file (and supporting files) to the proper site folder, located in the Sites folder of your iDisk.

Figure 4.63 After you've loaded the HTML file, the "Edit your page" page loads, allowing you to type a new name for your custom HTML page.

Figure 4.64 After you click the Preview button, the custom page loads as others would see it.

Figure 4.65 After you publish the custom HTML page, its URL is displayed in a Congratulations page, and you're given the opportunity to send an iCard announcing it.

Publishing a Custom Site Sans HomePage

If you're a stickler for keeping things organized, there's another way to host your custom site through your .Mac account that doesn't involve HomePage.

Rather than uploading the bare Web page and any supporting files for your custom site, upload the folder that contains those pages. There is one major benefit to doing it this way—you can keep your content organized by folder (staying out of the way of the HomePage application). Here's how you go about it.

1. Upload your entire custom site's folder to the Sites folder on your iDisk.

2. Log in to your .Mac account, and click the HomePage link.

3. Rather than clicking the Advanced tab, select the site where you want to include the new custom page, and click the Site Menu tab (**Figure 4.66**). On the new site-menu page that results, click the plus (+) button next to where you'd like a link to your custom site to appear. See the sidebar "Adding Links to Your Site Menu," earlier in this chapter, for complete instructions.

Figure 4.66 To create a new site menu, first select the site where you'd like the menu page to appear in the second column from the left, and then click the Site Menu tab below.

continues on next page

Publishing a Custom Site Sans HomePage *(continued)*

4. On the "Edit your links" page, click the Other Pages tab, and type in the URL for the index file inside your newly uploaded site folder (such as http://homepage.mac.com/dreynolds/webcam/webcam.html) (**Figure 4.67**).

5. Click Apply.

6. Click Preview to see how the site will look before it goes live. If you like what you see, click Publish.

You can edit an existing site-menu page in the same way to include the new site.

Also, here's one tip worth remembering: If you're using this technique, consider naming the index page inside the folder index.html. Why? Most Web servers, including the .Mac Web server, are set to automatically serve up the page named index.html if one isn't specified. So, that means that

http://homepage.mac.com/dreynolds/webcam/index.html

and

http://homepage.mac.com/dreynolds/webcam/

work the same. And, hey, you're doing your visitors a favor—a shorter URL means less typing for anyone who wants to visit your site.

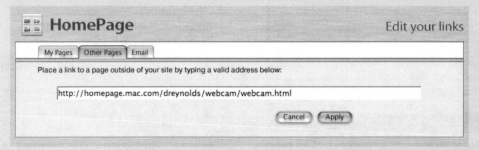

Figure 4.67 Create a link to the newly integrated site by entering its URL in the Other Pages field, and then click Apply.

USING iWEB WITH .MAC

5

In Chapter 4, we covered how to build Web pages using .Mac's built-in page-creation tool, HomePage (and, if you're the adventurous sort, how to integrate custom-built pages into your site).

If you're the proud owner of iLife '06, however, there is another way to create and share Web pages using your .Mac account. You can go beyond the templates that HomePage provides, without having to master HTML code or a hodgepodge of software tools. That's all thanks to iWeb, the newest member of Apple's iLife ensemble.

While HomePage provides a quick way to get Web pages posted on your .Mac account, iWeb is a full-fledged Web-page-creation application. You can use iWeb to create completely custom Web pages (and entire sites), and the best part of it is, you can *still* use its built-in templates to quickly build your pages without breaking a sweat.

We'll show you how to create pages using the iWeb templates and themes, and we'll go over how to manage one or more sites using iWeb.

Creating Pages

iWeb is all about creating elegant Web pages easily—the Apple way, of course. While iWeb can be used to create Web pages that are hosted on your .Mac account, with just a few clicks, it can do much more than that—much of which is beyond the scope of this book.

That said, publishing a page—a beautiful page—and posting it to .Mac is a two-step affair: creating a page from one of the templates, and then clicking the Publish button to copy it to .Mac. It's *that* simple.

We'll show you how to create a basic page and upload it to your .Mac site. If you want to know how to get the most out of iWeb, you'll need to check out a solid iLife book, such as *The Macintosh iLife '06*, by Jim Heid.

iWeb Site Management

While iWeb is great for creating individual Web pages, it's also very good at managing an entire site (at least one that you're likely to create at home). It automatically creates and maintains navigation links for all pages in a site.

To create a new site, choose File > New Site (or press Command-Shift-N), and then create a page for your new site. Every time you add a page to your site and publish it, the site's navigation is automatically updated.

Figure 5.1 iWeb features several themes for your pages and sites (left), and six templates plus a blank page for each theme.

Figure 5.2 The Welcome template serves as a lead-in to your Web site.

Figure 5.3 The About Me template provides guidance for posting your personal details.

Themes and Templates

The first time you launch iWeb, it invites you to choose a template for your new Web page (**Figure 5.1**), but in fact, you'll really have to do a little more than that: In the course of choosing a template, you'll also need to choose a *theme* for the Web site that the page will occupy (even if the site will consist of just one lone page). Sound complicated? Don't worry. It isn't.

Each of iWeb's professionally designed themes provides an overall "look" for your site, including a harmonious color scheme; complementary fonts for headings, body copy, and captions; and accents such as background images and picture borders. There are 18 themes to choose from, ranging from basic ("Black" and "White") to elegant ("Formal" and "Watercolor") to edgy with attitude ("Freestyle" and "Night Life"). Within each theme there are six templates, plus a blank page for pages with different purposes. As we'll discuss later, if the designers' purposes in creating the templates don't match yours, you can tweak your pages as much as you desire.

You can browse the iWeb site themes by scrolling through the thumbnails on the left side of the "Choose a template for your webpage" window. Click a theme thumbnail to see thumbnails of the templates for the pages you can create with it (see Figure 5.1). The following are the templates within each theme:

◆ **Welcome.** This template serves as an entry page to your site; each design option features a banner graphic and a big block of text (**Figure 5.2**).

◆ **About Me.** This template provides a way of putting out your personal information (**Figure 5.3**).

◆ **Photos.** This template makes it easy for you to build photo pages containing thumbnails (miniature photos that enlarge when clicked) and captions (**Figure 5.4**).

◆ **Movie.** This template provides shells for posting movie files, accompanied by explanatory text (**Figure 5.5**).

◆ **Blog.** A little tricky: This template provides a shell for a blog (short for *Web log*, or online journal), and each option features three separate Web-page designs: one for the blog's homepage, one for the main-entry page, and one for an archive of all entries (**Figure 5.6**).

Figure 5.4 The Photos template makes it easy to post your photographs to .Mac.

Figure 5.5 The Movie template gives you a place to post a video.

Figure 5.6 The Blog template lets you create a blog, complete with a homepage, an archive, and individual entries.

Figure 5.7 The Podcast template gives structure to your audio musings.

◆ **Podcast.** Designed for use in conjunction with GarageBand 3, iWeb's companion program in the Apple iLife '06 package, the Podcast template lets you publish your own "radio shows" to a .Mac Web site. Like the Blog template, each Podcast template consists of three page designs: one for your podcast's homepage, one for each individual entry, and one for an archive of all podcast entries (**Figure 5.7**).

◆ **Blank.** Fairly self-explanatory, this is an empty page based on the theme design, which you can fill up with anything you choose.

Although these pages have names that imply how they should be used, they don't *have* to be used this way. To a far greater extent than is possible with HomePage, iWeb lets you adapt the text and images within templates to make your pages into whatever you like. Just choose a theme and template that serves your needs, and you can customize that page however you like.

Before we get to that, let's try creating a basic Welcome page.

THEMES AND TEMPLATES

Create and Upload a Web Page

1. Open the iWeb application.

   The iWeb interface loads, showing the "Choose a template for your webpage" dialog (**Figure 5.8**).

2. If this dialog isn't displayed (as will be the case once you've already created a page with iWeb), choose File > New Page (or press Command-N).

3. In the dialog that appears, choose a theme from the column on the left (such as Black, White, or Formal), choose the Welcome template, and then click Choose (**Figure 5.9**).

   The template loads, complete with placeholder image and text.

Figure 5.8 When first loaded, iWeb asks you to choose a template for the page you're creating.

Figure 5.9 Pick a theme and the Welcome template, and then click Choose to get started.

Figure 5.10 Click the Media button to access all of your iLife content, such as music, movies, and pictures.

4. Click the Media button in the lower right corner of the window (**Figure 5.10**).

The Media Browser loads (**Figure 5.11**).

5. If it's not already selected, click the Photos tab in the Media Browser window.

Your iPhoto library is displayed (**Figure 5.12**).

continues on next page

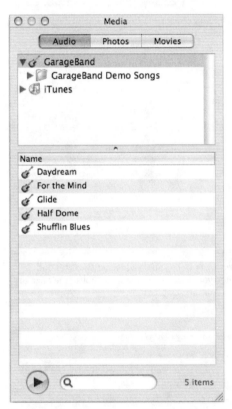

Figure 5.11 The Media Browser lists all of the music, movies, and photos available for posting on your Web page.

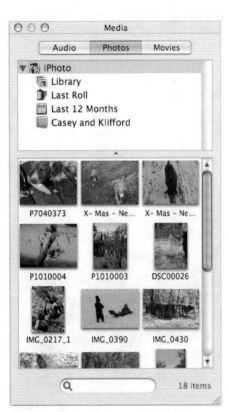

Figure 5.12 The Photos pane of the Media Browser displays all of the pictures in your iPhoto library.

CREATE AND UPLOAD A WEB PAGE

6. Drag the picture you want to use from the Media Browser to the placeholder picture in the template (**Figure 5.13**).

   Your picture is added to the page (**Figure 5.14**).

7. Double-click the text block and type in the text for your page.

   Your page is ready to go (**Figure 5.15**).

8. In the lower left portion of the window, click the Publish button.

   Your page is uploaded to your .Mac account, and a dialog slides down, offering three buttons: Announce, Visit Site Now, and OK (**Figure 5.16**).

Figure 5.14 When you drop a picture on the page, it takes the place of the placeholder image.

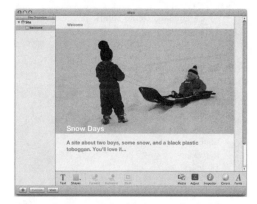

Figure 5.15 Once you've added your images and edited your text, you're ready to publish the page to your .Mac account.

Figure 5.16 After you've published a page to your .Mac account, you're given three options: Announce, Visit Site Now, or OK. Click the button for the option you want.

Figure 5.13 To put an image on your Web page, drag it from the Media Browser to the placeholder picture.

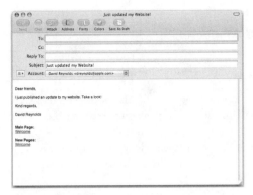

Figure 5.17 When you click Announce, an e-mail message is automatically generated in your preferred e-mail client. You can edit it, add e-mail addresses for the people you want to send it to, and then send it.

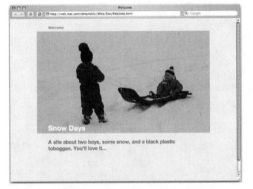

Figure 5.18 When you click Visit Site Now, your newly updated site is loaded in your Web browser.

Figure 5.19 When you click OK after publishing a page, you are returned to iWeb where you left it.

9. In the dialog, *click one of the following buttons:*

   ▲ Click Announce to automatically generate an e-mail message that you can send out to announce your new page and site (**Figure 5.17**).

   ▲ Click the Visit Site Now button to go directly to your new page (**Figure 5.18**).

   ▲ Click the OK button to return to work in iWeb (**Figure 5.19**).

✔ Tips

■ When you're working on a site that contains more than one page, clicking the Visit Site Now button takes you to that site's homepage, not necessarily the page you're working on. From there, follow links to the page you want to visit. The Visit button in the bottom-left corner of the iWeb window behaves the same way.

■ You don't *have* to use the Media Browser to add pictures to your page; it just makes the job easier. You can, in fact, drag an image from a Finder window onto your page for the same effect.

■ If you've set up your Mac with your .Mac account information, iWeb will automatically publish to your .Mac account with a click of the Publish button.

■ iWeb automatically updates the site's navigation bar, depending on what pages are in the site, using the pages' names. You don't have to do a thing!

■ To adjust your page to your liking (and control where the page is published), click the Inspector button to bring up the Inspector palette. (For more info on this, see sidebar, The Mysterious Inspector.)

The Mysterious Inspector

iWeb has a powerful and somewhat mysterious tool that lets you control items on the pages you create: the Inspector palette (**Figure 5.20**).

A complete discussion of iWeb and the Inspector is beyond the scope of this book (you'll find it covered in *The Macintosh iLife '06*, by Jim Heid). Still, it would be remiss to skip over the Inspector altogether. Consider this a brief introduction and an invitation to explore the Inspector in greater detail. To begin, click the Inspector button in the lower-right corner of the iWeb page (the one with an *i* on it). Then click an item on your page, and the selected item's attributes will be loaded into the Inspector window.

The attributes governed by the Inspector vary, depending on the nature of the object you select; settings available for images differ from those for text objects or movies, for example. But generally, the Inspector controls seven aspects of your Web sites, the pages within them, and the objects embedded in those pages; each of these aspects corresponds to one of the seven buttons arranged along the top edge of the palette.

Figure 5.20 The Inspector palette lets you control everything from the title of your site to the positioning of a picture on a page. This portion of the inspector shows the site's name, the group to which the page is published, and how much iDisk storage is left.

continues on next page

The Mysterious Inspector *(continued)*

Detailing all seven buttons, and the attributes they govern for various Web-page objects, would require a chapter unto itself, but the following list highlights the main functions of each button in the Inspector window, as they appear from left to right:

- **Site** (blue-orb icon) lets you give your site a name, choose whether your site is published to a group, and set a password for sites published to a .Mac account. This portion of the inspector also includes a Site tab for additional control over your site.

- **Page** (dogeared-page icon) allows you to set a name, fill color, and size for your page, as well as to decide whether the page is included in the site's navigation.

- **Blog & Podcast** ("RSS" icon) lets you choose how many excerpts (and the length of those excepts) are shown on a blog or podcast page, and lets you to specify podcast details (such as whether it requires a parental advisory and whether it should be listed in the iTunes Music Store).

- **Text** (capital "T" icon) provides fine-grained control over how the text on your page appears.

- **Graphic** (square-and-circle icon). controls image fill and stroke colors, and applies special image effects.

- **Metrics** (ruler icon) lets you control the exact size, rotation, and positioning of items on the page.

- **Link** (curved-arrow icon) permits you to quickly create hyperlinks on your pages.

Click around these buttons and study (or inspect) the attributes they govern, and before long, you'll get a feel for how the Inspector works.

Note that the Inspector is just one of several tool palettes you'll find in iWeb. Others include:

- **Media Browser.** Used extensively for many tasks detailed in this chapter, this palette lets you incorporate pictures, audio, and videos into your pages.

- **Adjust Image.** This palette lets you make changes to images on a page.

- **Colors.** This palette is used to assign colors to elements on the page. and finally;

- **Fonts.** This palette lets you exercise some control over the fonts on your page.

You can get at these palettes by clicking the respective buttons at the bottom of the main window, or selecting the appropriate items from the Window menu.

Create and Upload a Blog Page with iWeb

1. Follow steps 1 and 2 of "To create and upload a Web page with iWeb."

   The iWeb interface loads, showing the "Choose a template for your webpage" dialog (see Figure 5.8).

2. In the dialog, choose a theme from the column on the left (such as Black, White, or Formal), choose the Blog template, and then click Choose (**Figure 5.21**).

   The template loads, complete with place-holder image and text (**Figure 5.22**).

Figure 5.21 To create a blog page, you'll first need to choose a theme and the Blog template in the "Choose a template for your webpage" dialog.

Figure 5.22 The Blog template includes placeholder text and images, and it also puts both a main blog page and an archive page on your site, as shown in the Site Organizer column at the left of the window.

Figure 5.23 To open the Media Browser, click the Media button.

3. Click the Media button in the lower-right corner of the window (**Figure 5.23**).

The Media Browser loads (**Figure 5.24**).

4. If it's not already selected, click the Photos tab in the Media Browser window.

Your iPhoto library is displayed (**Figure 5.25**).

continues on next page

Figure 5.24 The Media Browser displays all of your iLife-related music, movies, and pictures.

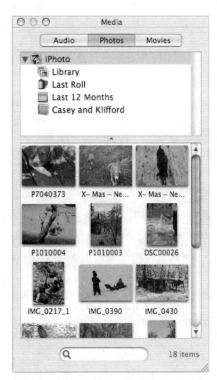

Figure 5.25 The Photos pane of the Media Browser shows your iPhoto library, complete with photo albums.

CREATE AND UPLOAD A BLOG PAGE WITH iWEB

5. Drag the picture you want to use from the Media Browser to the placeholder picture on the iWeb page (**Figure 5.26**).

Your picture is added to the page (**Figure 5.27**).

6. Double-click the text block, and type in the text for your page.

Your blog entry is ready to go (**Figure 5.28**).

Figure 5.27 After you drop an image on the page, it's automatically added.

Figure 5.26 When you drag an image onto your page, the pointer turns into a round green cursor with a plus (+) symbol and a number, indicating that you're adding an image to the page, as well as how many you're adding.

Figure 5.28 After you add custom pictures and edit the text to your liking, your page is ready to publish to your .Mac account.

Figure 5.29 When you create a blog page from a template, you also create a main blog page, which describes your blog and lists any entries. The page is preloaded with placeholder images and text.

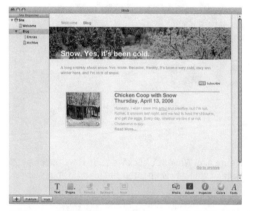

Figure 5.30 After you've customized your page by adding your own images and text, you're ready to publish it to your .Mac Web site.

7. In the Site Organizer column at the left side of the window, click the Blog item.

The main blog page loads (**Figure 5.29**).

8. Repeat steps 5 and 6 for this page, customizing your main blog page (you'll have to do this only once . . .) (**Figure 5.30**).

Your blog entry is uploaded to your .Mac account, the index of blog entries is updated and uploaded, the Archive page is updated and loaded, and a dialog slides down, offering three buttons: Announce, Visit Site Now, and OK.

continues on next page

9. In the dialog, *click one of the buttons:*

▲ Click Announce to automatically generate an e-mail message that you can send out to announce your new page and site (**Figure 5.31**).

▲ Click the Visit Site Now button to go directly to your new page (**Figure 5.32**).

▲ Click the OK button to return to work in iWeb (**Figure 5.33**).

✔ Tips

■ Creating a Photos page or About Me page is basically the same process: Make a new page, drop images on the page in the image placeholders, edit the text, and click Publish. It's that easy (except that the Photos page has more pictures).

■ Your blogs automatically generate an RSS feed that others can subscribe to.

■ You can change the name of your blog anytime by clicking Blog in the left-side Site Organizer column, and typing a new name when "Blog" is highlighted.

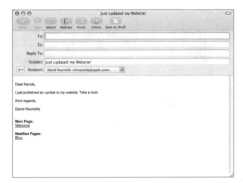

Figure 5.31 When you click Announce, an e-mail message is automatically generated in your preferred e-mail client. You can edit it, add e-mail addresses for the people you want to send it to, and then send it.

Figure 5.32 When you click Visit Site Now, the homepage of your newly updated site loads in your Web browser.

Figure 5.33 When you click OK after publishing a page, you are returned to iWeb just where you left it.

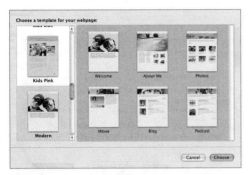

Figure 5.34 Choose a theme for your page (on the left), click Podcast for your template, and then click Choose.

Figure 5.35 The Podcast template contains placeholder text and images, as well as a placeholder for an audio file—the heart and soul of a podcast.

Create and Upload a Podcast Page

iWeb lets you join the monologue revolution by making it easy to post your own podcasts — "radio" shows you record as digital-audio files and post to the Web, where others can subscribe to them and get them downloaded to their computers automatically. The easiest way to do this is to use GarageBand 3, a companion to iWeb in Apple's iLife '06 application suite, but unfortunately detailing how is more than we can tackle in this book. If you read *The Macintosh iLife '06*, by Jim Heid, you'll get a handle on it quickly. With this task, we'll assume that you've already created a podcast audio file, and that it's in your iTunes directory.

1. Follow steps 1 and 2 of "To create and upload a Web page with iWeb."

   The iWeb interface loads, showing the "Choose a template for your webpage" dialog (see Figure 5.8).

2. In the dialog, choose a theme on the left (such as Black, White, or Formal), choose the Podcast template, and then click Choose (**Figure 5.34**).

   The template loads, complete with placeholder image and text (**Figure 5.35**).

continues on next page

3. Click the Media button in the lower right corner of the window (**Figure 5.36**).

The Media Browser loads (**Figure 5.37**).

4. If it's not already selected, click the Photos tab in the Media Browser window.

Your iPhoto library is displayed (**Figure 5.38**).

Figure 5.36 Click the Media button to open the Media Browser.

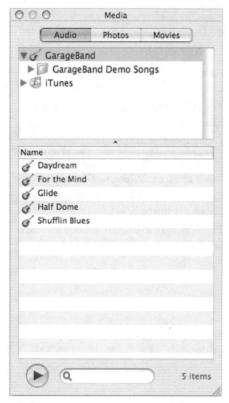

Figure 5.37 The Media Browser provides easy access to your iLife music, pictures, and movies.

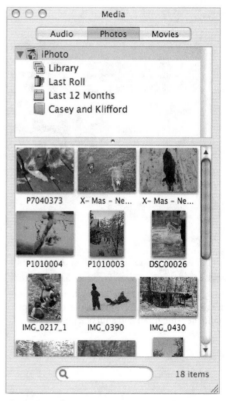

Figure 5.38 The Photos pane of the Media Browser shows your iPhoto library, complete with photo albums.

Figure 5.39 Drag the image you want to use as the banner for your Webcast from the Media Browser window to the placeholder banner image.

Figure 5.40 When it is dragged to the iWeb page, your image replaces the placeholder banner image.

5. Drag the picture you want to use from the Media Browser to the placeholder pictures on the iWeb page (**Figure 5.39**). Your picture is added to the page (**Figure 5.40**).

6. Click the Media Browser's Audio tab. Your GarageBand and iTunes libraries are displayed (**Figure 5.41**).

continues on next page

Figure 5.41 The Audio pane of the Media Browser shows your GarageBand creations, including podcasts, as well as your iTunes libraries and playlists.

7. Navigate to the audio file you want to use as your podcast, and drag it to the image above the audio track on the iWeb page.

   The audio file is included on your podcast page (**Figure 5.42**).

8. If it's not already selected, click the Photos tab in the Media Browser window.

   Your iPhoto library is displayed (see Figure 5.41).

9. Drag the picture you want to use from the Media Browser to the Drag Image Here placeholder (**Figure 5.43**).

   The picture is added to the page above the audio file (**Figure 5.44**).

Figure 5.43 To add an image to your now-empty image placeholder for your podcast, simply drag the image to the place that says "Drag Image Here"— simple, eh?

Figure 5.42 After you drag an audio file to your page, it appears there, ready for upload (it's the audio control below the Drag Image Here area of the window).

Figure 5.44 The picture you drag onto the image placeholder is added to your podcast page.

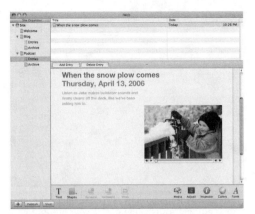

Figure 5.45 After updating your images, text, and audio file, you're ready to publish your page to your .Mac account.

Figure 5.46 Like a blog, your podcast has a main page that describes your general podcast, and lists podcast entries below it.

Figure 5.47 After uploading your podcast page, you're given the option of announcing it to those who are presumably interested, visiting the podcast page, or going on about your business in iWeb.

10. Double-click the text block and type in the text for your page.

Your podcast entry is ready to go (**Figure 5.45**).

11. In the Site Organizer column at the left of the window, click the Podcast item.

The main Podcast page loads (**Figure 5.46**).

12. Repeat steps 5 and 10 for this page, customizing your main podcast page (you'll have to do this only once . . .).

Your podcast entry is uploaded to your .Mac account, the index of blog entries is updated and uploaded, the Archive page is updated and loaded, and a dialog slides down, offering three buttons: Announce, Visit Site Now, and OK (**Figure 5.47**).

continues on next page

13. In the dialog, *click one of the following buttons:*

▲ Click Announce to automatically generate an e-mail message that you can send out to announce your new page and site (**Figure 5.48**).

▲ Click the Visit Site Now button to go directly to your new page (**Figure 5.49**).

▲ Click the OK button to return to work in iWeb (**Figure 5.50**).

✔ Tip

■ To submit your podcast to iTunes, choose File > Submit Podcast to iTunes, enter the requested information in the dialog that slides down, and then click Publish and Submit. This publishes the podcast to your .Mac account *and* submits it for publication on iTunes.

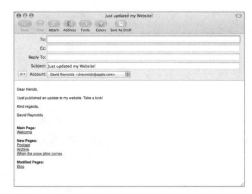

Figure 5.48 When you click Announce, an e-mail message is automatically generated in your preferred e-mail client. You can edit it, add e-mail addresses for the people you want to send it to, and then send it.

Figure 5.49 When you click Visit Site Now, your newly updated podcast index page loads in your Web browser.

Figure 5.50 When you click OK after publishing a page, you are returned to iWeb just where you left it.

Figure 5.51 The first step in enabling comments on your site is to select one of its pages (any one of them) in iWeb.

Enable Comments in iWeb

As this book was going to press, Apple released a free iWeb update, version 1.1, which added several cool new features to the program, including extra themes and templates as well as support for letting visitors search your blog and podcast sites. As with all the features of the "original" iWeb, describing every version-1.1. addition is beyond the scope of this book, but one new feature—support for reader comments on blog and podcast sites—is too cool to leave out.

Comments support lets you transform your blog or podcast from a speech to a conversation. It lets visitors respond to your posts with questions, observations, and even rebuttals. You can use comments yourself to answer your audience, and visitors can also talk among themselves about how much they admire your brilliant insights.

Here's an overview of how to enable comments on your site, and how to get rid of them in case you're extremely modest or the debate gets a little too heated:

To activate comments in a blog or podcast

1. You can't enable comments in a blog or podcast until the blog or podcast site exists. So if you haven't already done so, follow the instructions in the preceding sections of this chapter to create an appropriate site.

2. Open the iWeb application and highlight the name of the index, entries, or archive page for your blog or podcast (**Figure 5.51**).

   Comment activation applies globally to every page in a site, so the specific page you choose isn't important.

   Click the Inspector button (the blue circle with "i" in the middle).

continues on next page

3. The Inspector palette opens.

Click RSS; in the RSS pane click the Blog tab (**Figure 5.52**) and check the "Allow comments" box.

4. The first time you enable comments for a blog or podcast, a confirmation dialog appears, explaining what you're about to do (**Figure 5.53**).

Check the "Don't show again" box if you don't want to see this reminder in the future, then click OK.

5. In the Blog pane, the "Allow attachments" check box, which was grayed out when "Allow comments" was unchecked, is now available. Check it if you'd like to allow site visitors to attach images, sound clips, or other files up to 5 MB in size to their comments (**Figure 5.54**).

Figure 5.52 Locate the "Allow comments" check box by clicking the RSS button in the iWeb Inspector, and then clicking the Blog tab.

Figure 5.53 The Allow Comments confirmation dialog makes sure you understand what you're doing.

Figure 5.54 Once "Allow comments" is checked, the "Allow attachments" check box becomes accessible.

Figure 5.55 If you check "Allow attachments," iWeb displays a cautionary dialog to make sure you understand what you've done.

6. The first time you check "Allow attachments," a dialog appears, explaining that any attachments posted to your site will be stored on your iDisk (**Figure 5.55**). Once again, check "Don't show again" if you don't want to see this reminder in the future, and then click OK.

7. Click the Publish button in the lower left corner of the iWeb window to re-post your site with Comments enabled, and attachments allowed if you opted for that.

To post or respond to comments

The processes of posting comments to your blog and responding to comments posted there are the same for you and your audience.

1. To add and respond to comments, you must be viewing your site in a Web browser. If you're editing the site in iWeb, click the Visit button in the lower left corner of the iWeb window. Otherwise, point your browser to your site's index page, http://web.mac.com/ *membername*/iWeb/*sitename* (replacing *membername* and *sitename* with your .Mac user name and (what else?) the site name.

   Navigate to the entry with the comment you want to address and click the Add a Comment link (**Figure 5.56**).

2. In the Add Comment window that appears (**Figure 5.57**), *do the following:*

   ▲ Type your remarks in the large Comment field.

   ▲ If an Add Attachment link appears below the Comment field and you'd like to post a file (photo, audio clip, or what have you) up to 5 MB in size along with your comment, click Add Attachment and then the Choose File button (**Figure 5.58**).

   ▲ Next, enter your name (or your *nom de blog*) in the "Comment as" field, and optionally add a URL for your homepage or any other Web site you care to be associated with.

   ▲ Finally, type the random five-character sequence displayed in the bottom-left image into the Image Verification field to its right. This is a required test to prove you're a human being, not an automated spam generator (which wouldn't be able to see and read the characters).

Figure 5.56 To add a comment to a blog, or respond to comments made by site visitors, view the site in a browser and click the Add a Comment link.

Figure 5.57 The Add Comment window lets you type in your remarks, prompts you for an ID and an optional Web link, and makes you prove you're not a spam-generating robot (which you probably already know).

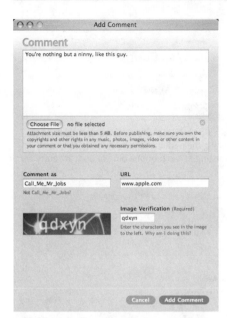

Figure 5.58 On sites with comment attachments enabled, clicking the Add Attachment link below the Comment field exposes the Choose File button, used to select an attachment file.

Figure 5.59 Clicking the Add Comment button at the bottom right summons the "Adding comment" progress pane, which stays until your comment and any attachment are posted to the site.

3. Click the Add Comment button to post your remarks and any attachments. The Adding Comment progress pane appears and stays until the page and any attachments have been posted to the site (**Figure 5.59**).

To delete comments from your site

Maybe you're having second thoughts about a response you posted to one of your audience members; maybe the discussion between posters is getting a tad too personal; or maybe you just want revel in your absolute power over your online domain. Whatever the case, you can remove any or all comments from your blog any time you like. Here's how.

1. Steer a Web browser to your site, by clicking click the Visit button for a relevant page in the lower left corner of the iWeb window, or by typing your site's URL into the browser address field: http://web. mac.com/*membername*/iWeb/*sitename* (replacing *membername* and *sitename* with your .Mac user name and site name, respectively).

   Navigate to the entry that houses the comment(s) you want to delete.

2. Locate the comment counter at the bottom of the main entry on the page (which indicates that there have been some number *n* comments to your post) and click the padlock icon next to it (**Figure 5.60**).

3. In the Site Owner Login screen that appears, type your .Mac member name and password into the appropriate fields (**Figure 5.61**).

4. In the Manage Comments screen that appears locate the comment(s) you want to delete.

   Check the boxes to the left of the comments you want to zap and click either Delete button; there's one at the top and another at the bottom of the window. When you've finished, click the Return to Entry link (**Figure 5.62**).

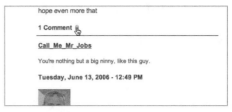

Figure 5.60 To delete an unwanted comment, begin by clicking the padlock icon next to the comment-count listing at the foot of a blog or podcast entry.

Figure 5.61 Type your .Mac member name and account password in the Site Owner Login dialog.

Figure 5.62 Check the boxes to the left of any comment(s) you want to remove, click either of the Delete buttons, and then click the Return to Entry Page link to go back to your site.

Figure 5.63 You can password-protect a site by opening it in iWeb, clicking the Site button in the Inspector, clicking the Password tab, and checking Make my published site private. Add a user name and password different from your .Mac member name and password.

✔ Tips

- If you want to delete all comments for an entry, you can select them all easily by checking one of the Select All boxes to the top left and bottom left of the Manage Comments page.

- If you find yourself having to trash nuisance posts all the time, consider password-protecting your site, so that only people you authorize can see it and post comments to it. To do so, open the site in iWeb, launch the Inspector, and click its Site button (the blue orb) and the Password tab (**Figure 5.63**).

Create and Upload a Movie Page

1. Follow steps 1 and 2 of "To create and upload a Web page with iWeb."

   The iWeb interface loads, showing the "Choose a template for your webpage" dialog (see Figure 5.8).

2. In the dialog, choose a theme from the column on the left (such as Black, White, or Formal), choose the Movie template, and then click Choose (**Figure 5.64**).

   The template loads, complete with place-holder image and text (**Figure 5.65**).

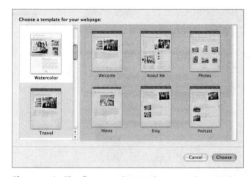

Figure 5.64 The first step in creating a movie page is to select a theme on the left and the Movie template on the right.

Figure 5.65 The Movie template is filled with a placeholder movie and text that you'll replace with your own content.

Figure 5.66 Click the Media button to open the Media Browser.

3. Click the Media button in the lower right corner of the window (**Figure 5.66**). The Media Browser opens (**Figure 5.67**).

4. If it's not already selected, click the Movies tab in the Media Browser window. The contents of the Movies folder in your home folder are displayed (**Figure 5.68**).

continues on next page

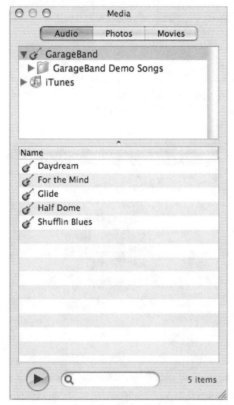

Figure 5.67 When you open the Media Browser, it may not show the media that you want to include on your page.

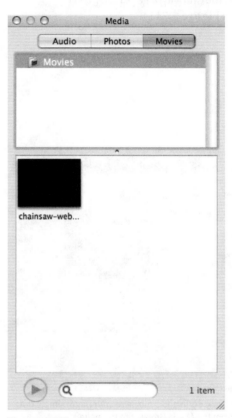

Figure 5.68 The Movies pane of the Media Browser shows all movies in your Movies folder.

CREATE AND UPLOAD A MOVIE PAGE

5. Drag the movie you want to use from the inspector to the placeholder movie in the iWeb page (**Figure 5.69**).

Your movie is added to the page (**Figure 5.70**).

6. Double-click the placeholder text blocks on the page, and type in the text you want to use.

Your movie page is ready to go (**Figure 5.71**).

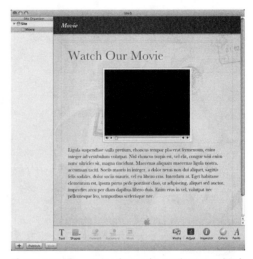

Figure 5.70 After you've dragged a movie to your iWeb page, it appears there, ready to be uploaded.

Figure 5.69 To add a movie to your page, simply drag it from the Media Browser to the page.

Figure 5.71 Once you've added your movie and edited the text, your page is ready to publish.

Figure 5.72 After you've uploaded your movie, iWeb lets you tell folks about it, visit the new page, or go back to iWeb.

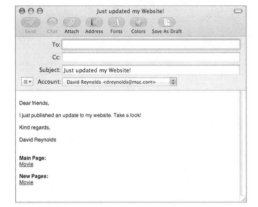

Figure 5.73 When you click Announce, an e-mail message is automatically generated in your preferred e-mail client. You can edit it, add e-mail addresses for the people you want to send it to, and then send it.

7. Click the Publish button.

Your movie page (along with the movie itself) is uploaded to your .Mac account, and a dialog slides down, offering three buttons: Announce, Visit Site Now, and OK (**Figure 5.72**).

8. In the dialog, *click one of the following buttons:*

▲ Click Announce to automatically generate an e-mail message that you can send out to announce your new page and site (**Figure 5.73**).

▲ Click the Visit Site Now button to go directly to your new page (**Figure 5.74**).

▲ Click the OK button to return to work in iWeb (**Figure 5.75**).

continues on next page

Figure 5.74 When you click Visit Site Now, your newly updated page is loaded in your Web browser.

Figure 5.75 When you click OK after publishing a page, you are returned to iWeb just where you left it.

CREATE AND UPLOAD A MOVIE PAGE

✔ Tips

- To see movies in the Media Browser window, create them in iMovie 3 and save them in the Movies folder.

- If you take movies with a digital still camera, you'll find those files in iPhoto, using the Photos tab of the Media Browser.

USING iPHOTO WITH .MAC

If you've purchased your Mac recently (or you've forked over the ridiculously low price for an iLife purchase), you have iLife '06 on your hard drive—and that means iPhoto 6. While earlier versions of iPhoto worked well with a .Mac account, iPhoto 6 takes this integration to a whole new level with two new talents: integration with iWeb, and creation of something that Apple calls *Photocasts*.

With iWeb integration, you can quickly create a photo page or photo-based set of blog entries without resorting to a lick of HTML—nice, even for those of you who don't mind getting dirty with tags and a text editor.

And, with the new Photocasting features, you can publish full-size photos to albums on your .Mac account and let others *subscribe* to them: Using iPhoto, Safari RSS, or another RSS reader, subscribers will be shown new pictures automatically, any time you add them to an album.

Using iPhoto with iWeb

Thanks to Apple's hard work at integrating iPhoto and iWeb, you can post two kinds of Web pages to your .Mac account using nothing but iPhoto (with iWeb in the background): a photo page, and a photo blog. *Blog* (short for *Web log*) is a fancy word for a Web page organized in a sort of diary format.

To create a photo page:

1. Open iPhoto 6.

   The main iPhoto interface is displayed (**Figure 6.1**).

2. Select the photos you want to use in the photo page and move them to their own album (**Figure 6.2**).

3. At the bottom of the page, select Photo Page from the iWeb button menu (**Figure 6.3**).

   iPhoto prepares the image files and then launches iWeb, which presents you with a choice of photo page templates (**Figure 6.4**).

Figure 6.1 iPhoto 6 lets you manage your digital photographs with ease, and it's very well integrated with your .Mac account.

Figure 6.2 Creating a new album with just the images you want to use in your picture page isn't absolutely required, but it helps you keep your page clean.

Figure 6.3 From the toolbar at the bottom of the page, select Photo Page from the iWeb button menu.

Figure 6.4 After iPhoto opens, choose the template you want to use for your photo page.

Figure 6.5 Your new photo page appears in iWeb, complete with the selected photos, but sporting placeholder text.

Figure 6.6 Replace the placeholder text on the page with the text you want others to see.

4. From the list to the left, pick a template that you like, and click Choose.

iWeb creates a page using the template, and populates it with your pictures and some placeholder text (**Figure 6.5**).

5. Double-click each text block (the title, description, and caption for each picture), and type the text you want to appear on the page (**Figure 6.6**).

continues on next page

6. In the lower left corner of the page, click the Publish button.

iWeb logs in to your .Mac account and uploads your Web page. After this is finished, you are notified that your page has been published (**Figure 6.7**).

7. *Choose one of the following by clicking the appropriate button:*

▲ **Announce.** Opens your e-mail program and sets up an announcement e-mail, prepopulated with the site's URL, some sample text, and a subject.

▲ **Visit Site Now.** Takes you directly to the site you just created.

▲ **OK.** Finishes the process and returns you to iWeb.

✔ Tip

■ You can use the iWeb Inspector to make changes to the appearance of your Photo pages. (For an overview of the Inspector, see The Mysterious Inspector sidebar in Chapter 5.)

Figure 6.7 The publication dialog gives you three options after publishing a page: announce it, visit it, or just go on about your business.

Figure 6.8 Click a photo thumbnail and select Blog from the iWeb button menu.

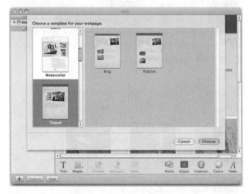

Figure 6.9 Choose a theme and template from the list presented by iWeb.

Figure 6.10 The blog page loads, showing the selected picture and some placeholder text.

To create a photo blog page:

1. Open iPhoto 6.

   The main iPhoto interface is displayed (see Figure 6.1).

2. Select a photo you want to use as the picture for your photo blog page, and from the iWeb button menu select Blog (**Figure 6.8**).

   The photo is prepared, and iWeb launches. If you haven't previously set up a blog in iWeb, the template-selection dialog will be displayed (**Figure 6.9**).

   If you've already got an iWeb blog, you won't see the template selection; the new page will be added as a new entry to the blog, using the design template you chose when you set up the blog. If you've set up more than one iWeb blog, you'll be prompted to choose from a pop-up menu the blog to which you want to add the new page. In either of these cases, skip to step 4 below and continue.

3. From the list to the left, choose a theme, and then pick a template, and click Choose. iWeb uses the template to create a separate blog entry page for each picture and populates them with placeholder text (**Figure 6.10**).

   continues on next page

4. Double-click each text block (the title, description, and caption for each picture), and type the text you want to appear on the page (**Figure 6.11**).

5. Click the Publish button (**Figure 6.12**). iWeb logs in to your .Mac account and uploads your Web page. After this is finished, you are notified that your page has been published (**Figure 6.13**).

6. *Choose one of the following by clicking the appropriate button:*

   ▲ **Announce.** Opens your e-mail program and sets up an announcement e-mail, prepopulated with the site's URL, some sample text, and a subject.

   ▲ **Visit Site Now.** Takes you directly to the site you just created.

   ▲ **OK.** Finishes the process and returns you to iWeb.

✔ Tips

- If you select more than one picture in iPhoto before choosing Blog from the iWeb button menu, iWeb will create a separate blog entry page for each picture. But be forewarned: It's a *lot* of work to customize each page.

- You can use the iWeb Inspector to tweak the appearance of your Photo Blog pages. (For a short introduction to this formidable tool, see The Mysterious Inspector sidebar in Chapter 5.)

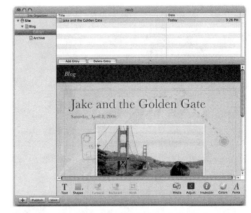

Figure 6.11 Replace the placeholder text on the page with the text you want visitors to see. Pictured here are the title and date, but there's also a description farther down the page.

Figure 6.12 Click the Publish button to publish your page to your .Mac account.

Figure 6.13 The notification dialog that opens after you publish a page gives you three options: announce the page, visit the page, or just continue working.

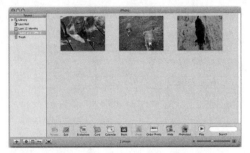

Figure 6.14 To create a Photocast, you must first create an album that contains the images you want to publish.

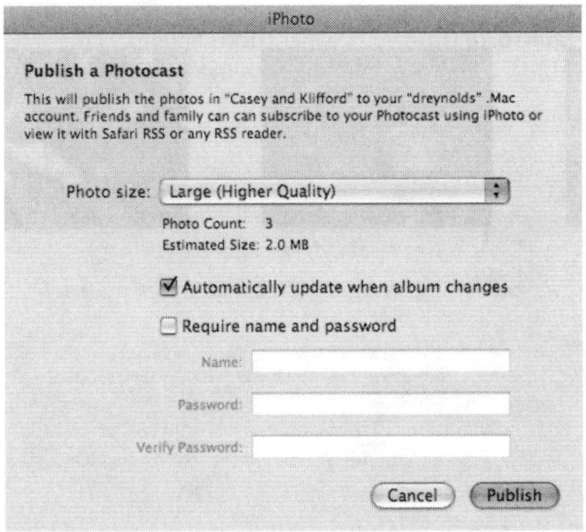

Figure 6.15 The Publish a Photocast dialog lets you decide how your Photocast will behave.

Working with Photocasts

iPhoto '06 includes a pretty nifty way to share full-resolution photos using your .Mac account, and Apple has dubbed this feature *Photocasting*. Aside from the attempt to ride the cultural wave of podcasting, creating a Photocast is simple and pretty cool.

A Photocast uploads pictures at full resolution (or lower resolutions, if you like) from iPhoto to your .Mac account, along with an accompanying RSS file. RSS (short for *Real Simple Syndication*) lets others subscribe to this Photocast (either with Safari RSS or an RSS reader that handles photos). Each subscriber gets the full-size versions of those pictures right in iPhoto (or a photo-compatible RSS reader), and the subscription is updated every time you add a photo to your Photocasted album—super for fellow Mac users with iPhoto 6.

To create a Photocast:

1. In iPhoto 6, create an album that contains the photos you want to Photocast.

   The photos in the album are displayed (**Figure 6.14**).

2. On the right side of the toolbar at the bottom of the page, click the Photocast button.

   The Publish a Photocast dialog slides down (**Figure 6.15**).

continues on next page

WORKING WITH PHOTOCASTS

3. In the Publish a Photocast dialog, *do the following:*

   ▲ Select a photo size (small, medium, large, or actual size) from the "Photo size" pop-up menu.

   ▲ Check the "Automatically update when album changes" box if you want the Photocast to be updated when the album is changed.

   ▲ Check the "Require name and password" box if you want the Photocast to be protected by a name and password. If you check this box, enter a name in the Name field, and enter the same password in both the Password and Verify Password fields.

   The Publish a Photocast dialog is complete (**Figure 6.16**).

4. Click the Publish button.

   The photos and generated RSS file are uploaded to your .Mac account, and a dialog appears, telling you that your album has been published (**Figure 6.17**).

5. In the dialog, *choose one of the following by clicking the respective button:*

   ▲ **Announce Photocast.** Click this button to generate an e-mail in your e-mail program that announces your Photocast, complete with a clickable URL for subscribers (**Figure 6.18**).

   ▲ **OK.** This returns you to iPhoto without doing anything else.

✔ Tip

■ The URLs for these pages can be awfully long, so it's worth looking at *redirection services* such as www.tinyurl.com. These services let you take a long URL and turn it into a short one for easy distribution.

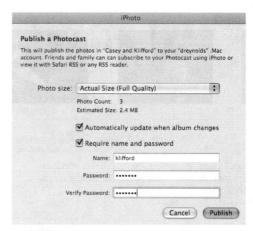

Figure 6.16 Once you've made the changes to the Publish a Photocast dialog, click the Publish button.

Figure 6.17 Once you've published your Photocast, you can choose between announcing the Photocast and going on about your business.

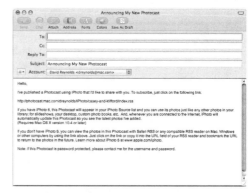

Figure 6.18 If you choose to announce your Photocast, an e-mail message is created in your e-mail program.

Figure 6.19 If you receive a Photocast invitation e-mail, simply click the link to launch iPhoto 6.

Figure 6.20 Once iPhoto has launched, it asks if you want to subscribe to the Photocast. Click the Subscribe button to do the deed.

Figure 6.21 Once you've subscribed to the Photocast, it appears as an album in your iPhoto Source list. For the curious, the album appears here twice—the first (with the circle with arrows in it) is the Photocast that's being published; the second (with the radiating semi-circles) is the subscribed Photocast. If someone subscribes to the Photocast, only the second album (and its accompanying icon) will appear.

To subscribe to a Photocast with iPhoto 6:

1. In the invitation e-mail, click the link (**Figure 6.19**).

   iPhoto launches, and a dialog slides down, asking if you want to subscribe (**Figure 6.20**).

2. Click the Subscribe button.

   iPhoto creates an album for the Photocast and downloads the images (**Figure 6.21**).

✔ Tips

- You (and your subscribers) don't have to use iPhoto or Safari RSS to subscribe to a Photocast. Other RSS applications work fine as well. Simply paste the URL from the invitation into the URL field of your RSS reader and bookmark it.

- To update a Photocast manually, click the sync icon (the circle with two half-circle arrows) next to its album icon in your iPhoto Source list. If you've subscribed to more than one Photocast, you'll find a single icon that syncs all of them next to the Photocasts folder icon in the Source list.

- Deleting a Photocast is easy: Simply select the Photocasted album in iPhoto, click the Photocast button, and then click the Stop Publishing button in the dialog that slides down. The Photocast will be removed from your .Mac account.

continues on next page

- Don't worry about memorizing the cumbersome URLs for your Photocasts (or stockpiling copies of the emails you send to announce them). If you need a reminder, highlight an album you've photocast in iPhoto's Source list and click the Information button (the "i" in a blue circle) in the lower-left corner of the iPhoto window. The URL will be displayed, though you probably won't be able to see all of it; you can stretch the Source window to see it all, or Option-click to copy the URL to the Clipboard.

- Besides sharing pictures with others, Photocasts provide a great way to synchronize iPhoto albums and libraries on two or more of your own Macs: Publish photos you add to one of the Macs as a Photocast and subscribe to it on your other Mac(s). Once the album you've subscribed to updates fully, delete it from your iPhoto Source list, but when prompted, choose to copy its contents to your local iPhoto library. Repeat with any other Macs you want to sync with, then you can Stop Publishing from the source Mac.

USING .MAC GROUPS

Some would say that the Internet is all about connecting with other people (that is, those who aren't busy saying the Internet is for comparison-shopping insurance). That's been true since the first e-mail messages started flitting around the ether (before spam ruined all that). These days, coordinating and connecting with a group takes more than e-mail alone—it takes custom Web pages, message boards, and more.

That's where .Mac groups come in. With them, you can create a group Web page, set up a message board, maintain a group calendar, and have a group e-mail address—all using your .Mac account. This is great for coordinating book clubs, sports teams, family activities, and even people who like to play the same video games as you do.

In this chapter, you'll learn how to set up a group, send messages using the group e-mail address, invite others to join your group, use the group iDisk space, post messages to your group message board, manage your group calendar, and delete a group once it's outlived its usefulness (or you really *need* to free up some iDisk space).

✔ Tip

- To get the skinny on .Mac groups from the proverbial horse's mouth, visit www. mac.com/1/Groups_faq.html.

Setting Up a Group

The first step in using your .Mac account to host a group site is to create it (go figure), which means you'll need to supply the following:

◆ A name for your group

◆ A group e-mail address (you get to make this up, but it'll end in @groups.apple.com)

◆ A group description

◆ Your group's time zone

You'll also need to pick a color scheme for your group and choose whether group members can *refer* others to your group—that is, invite new recruits to sign up.

✔ Tip

■ To create a group on your .Mac account, you must have at least 30 MB of iDisk space available. You also need a full .Mac membership (not a trial version).

To create a group:

1. In your Web browser, navigate to www.mac.com.
   The main .Mac page loads (**Figure 7.1**).

2. Click the Groups link in the navigation bar.
   The .Mac login page loads (**Figure 7.2**).

3. Type your .Mac member name and password, then click Login.
   The main .Mac groups page loads (**Figure 7.3**).

Figure 7.1 The main .Mac page is what the world sees when it visits www.mac.com.

Figure 7.2 Enter your member name and password, and then click Login to log in to your .Mac account.

Figure 7.3 If you've logged in by clicking the Groups link and you don't have any groups, you are presented with the main .Mac groups page that describes what groups are all about.

4. Click the "Create a group" button.

The "Set up your group" page loads (**Figure 7.4**).

continues on next page

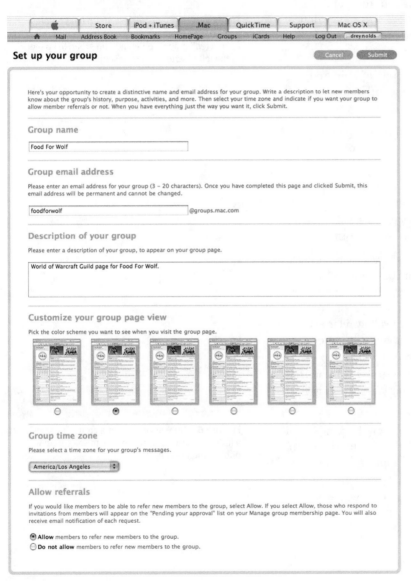

Figure 7.4 On the group setup page, you can give your group a name, assign it an e-mail address, create a description, choose a color scheme, select a time zone, and decide whether or not to allow referrals. Once you've filled in all of the personal details, click the Submit button.

5. *Do the following:*

▲ In the "Group name" field, type your group's name.

▲ In the "Group email address" field, type the e-mail address you'd like to use. Remember—this can be done only once and can't be changed, so use care.

▲ In the "Description of your group" field, type a description for your group.

▲ In the "Customize your group page view" area, choose one of the six color schemes.

▲ From the "Group time zone" popup menu, select a time zone for your group's messages. This will be used to time-stamp group postings.

▲ In the "Allow referrals" section, click the "Allow" or "Do not allow" radio button to select whether group members can invite other people to join the group. (If you allow referrals, you, as group owner, can still approve or deny any new members.)

Click the Submit button; your group list page loads, showing your new group (**Figure 7.5**).

6. Click the right arrow on the right side of the page, or click the URL for the group's main page, which appears under the group's title.

The group page loads the way others will see it (**Figure 7.6**). It's a little plain, but we can change that.

Figure 7.5 When you create a group (and before you assign an image), you'll see the generic "Get connected" graphic on your main group list page, to the left of your group's description.

Figure 7.6 After you've created a group, its page looks a little plain. Don't worry—you can spice it up with photos and messages.

Figure 7.7 Click the "Add an image" link to add a picture to your page.

Figure 7.8 After you click the "Add an image" link, you'll see controls for uploading an image to your group.

To customize your group page:

1. In the left column just below the generic .Mac Groups image, click the "Add an image" link (**Figure 7.7**).

    The column expands down to show controls for adding an image (**Figure 7.8**).

2. Click the Choose File button.

    A file-selection dialog slides down (**Figure 7.9**).

3. In the file-selection dialog, navigate to the GIF or JPEG image you want to use, select it, and then click Choose.

    The filename appears to the right of the Choose File button (**Figure 7.10**).

continues on next page

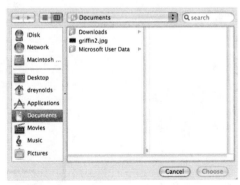

Figure 7.9 In the file-selection dialog, choose the graphic you want to upload to your group page.

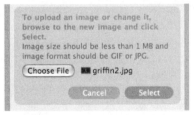

Figure 7.10 After you've uploaded an image to your group, its name appears to the right of the Choose File button. Click Select to continue.

SETTING UP A GROUP

4. Click the Select button.

The page reloads, showing the image you uploaded (**Figure 7.11**).

5. In the Photos section of the page, click the "Add photos" link (**Figure 7.12**).

Your group iDisk page loads in a new window, and a login dialog slides down (**Figure 7.13**).

6. Type your member name and password in the respective fields and click Log In.

The GroupSlideshow folder in the group iDisk page finishes loading (**Figure 7.14**).

Figure 7.12 Click the "Add photos" link in the Photos section to upload photos to your group.

Figure 7.13 Before you can access your group iDisk, you have to enter your .Mac member name and password, and then click Log In to continue.

Figure 7.11 After you upload an image to your group, it appears in the upper left corner of the page.

Figure 7.14 Your group's slide-show folder on the group iDisk page loads, showing any files there. Since we're creating our slide show, we don't have any—yet.

Figure 7.15 Use the "Select a file to upload" feature to upload images for your group slide show.

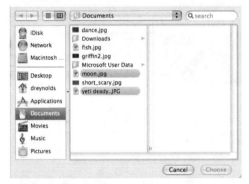

Figure 7.16 Choose the image that you want to upload for your slide show.

Figure 7.17 After you've uploaded an image to your group's iDisk, its name appears to the right of the Choose File button.

Figure 7.18 Now that you've uploaded a file to your group's slide-show portion of the iDisk, it's listed in the iDisk window.

7. In the upper right corner, click the Upload button.

   A "Select a file to upload" dialog opens (**Figure 7.15**).

8. Click the Choose File button.

   A file-selection dialog slides down (**Figure 7.16**).

9. In the file-selection dialog, navigate to the first picture that you'll be uploading to the slide show, and then click Choose.

   The file's name appears to the right of the Choose File button (**Figure 7.17**).

10. Click the Upload button.

    The picture is uploaded to the group iDisk in the GroupSlideshow folder. The page reloads showing the image (**Figure 7.18**).

continues on next page

11. Repeat steps 7–10 for each image file (up to a total of 99) that you want to upload for your slide show.

The files are listed in the window (**Figure 7.19**).

12. Close the iDisk window.

You are returned to your main group window (**Figure 7.20**).

13. Refresh the browser window.

Your slide show is now displayed in the upper right portion of the window (**Figure 7.21**).

You've now created a group and customized the main portions of the interface.

✔ Tips

■ Once you've created (or joined) a group, clicking the Groups item in the .Mac navigation bar will take you to a page that lists your groups and gives you the option to set up a new group.

■ You can bypass your .Mac page and log in to a group page directly by aiming a Web browser at the URL http://groups.mac.com/*groupname*, replacing *groupname* with the short name of your group. You can get this URL on your groups list page. When you create a group, you give it a name, often with more than one word. But that doesn't work so well for e-mail addresses and URLs. So, when you create a group name (such as *My fabulous group*), it gets shortened to *myfabulousgroup* for purposes of URLs and e-mail addresses. That's your short group name.

Figure 7.19 Five images have been uploaded to your group's slide-show folder and are listed here.

Figure 7.20 After you've uploaded images for your slide show, you are returned to your main group page. However, your slide show doesn't display yet.

Figure 7.21 Once you refresh your page, the images you uploaded are displayed.

Figure 7.22 When you log in to your .Mac account and click the Groups navigation element, all of your active groups are listed.

Figure 7.23 The group page shows everything you've set up so far for your group.

Managing Group Members

Army recruiting slogans aside, a group of one, such as the one you just created, isn't really a group. The solution? Use the group membership tools to invite others to join your group. And if you need to remove a few members from your group (say they move away and no longer play city league softball), the membership tools can do that, too.

To invite others to your group:

1. Log in to your .Mac account following steps 1–3 of "To create a group."

   Your "My groups" page loads (**Figure 7.22**).

2. On the right side of the group, click the right-pointing arrow.

   The group's page loads (**Figure 7.23**).

   continues on next page

3. In the lower left portion of the page in the Members section, click the Invite link.

The "Invite new members" page loads (**Figure 7.24**).

4. *Do the following* (**Figure 7.25**):

▲ For each person you want to add, type the person's first name, last name, and e-mail address in the appropriate fields.

▲ If you need to invite more than four people, click the plus (+) button next to "Add another row" below the last row of names and e-mail addresses.

▲ Type a personal invitation in the "Personal message" text box.

▲ Click the Continue button.

A preview of your invitation appears (**Figure 7.26**).

5. If you want to edit the invitation, click the Back button.

The "New member invitation" page reloads (see Figure 7.27).

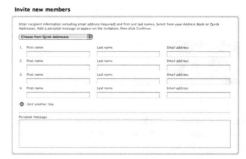

Figure 7.24 The "Invite new members" page allows you to fill in the blanks pertaining to those you want to invite.

Figure 7.25 After you've filled in the details for the people you want to invite, you're ready to issue your invitations by clicking Continue.

Figure 7.26 Before you send out your invitation, you're given the opportunity to review it and make changes.

Figure 7.27 Check the "Send me a copy" box to have a copy of the invitation sent to your .Mac e-mail address.

New member invitation

Your invitation(s) have been sent.

Figure 7.28 Once you've sent an invitation, you're given a confirmation that it's on its way.

6. If you want to have a copy of the invitation sent to you, check the "Send me a copy" box (**Figure 7.27**).

7. If the invitation looks OK, click the Send button.

A page loads telling you that the invitation has been sent (**Figure 7.28**).

8. Click the "Back to group" button to return to the main group page.

✔ Tips

- If you see a blue Invite link at the bottom of your group's member list, the group owner has authorized you to refer others to the group. Click the link to issue an e-mail invitation, but remember that the group owner must approve all new members.

- To send an invitation to a contact in your Quick Addresses list, pick a name from the Choose from Quick Addresses popup menu at the top of the page. The address will be automatically added to the next empty row. (For more on using Quick Addresses, see Chapter 2, "Sending Mail.")

- Although the owner of a group must have a paid .Mac membership, other group members do not. Each group member must have a .Mac ID, however. A .Mac ID is assigned to anyone age 13 or older (even users of Windows PCs) who signs up for a free .Mac trial subscription at www.mac. com. Even after their 60-day trials expire, members can still use their .Mac IDs to log in to group pages. If you invite someone without a .Mac ID to join a group, the invitation e-mail will guide him or her to an ID sign-up page.

- Invitations to join groups expire after 30 days. Anyone who waits that long before accepting will be prompted to send you an e-mail requesting a new invitation.

Accepting an Invitation

If someone has invited you to join a .Mac group, it's easy to accept that invitation. Your invite will arrive in the form of an e-mail with a personal message and a "Join group now" button (**Figure 7.29**).

To join the group, click the "Join group now" button. You can use your existing .Mac member ID to accept the invitation. If you don't have one, you'll be taken to a page where you can sign up for one.

To manage members:

Once you've created a group and people have joined it, you may need to add a few more, or say good-bye to some. That's where managing members comes in handy.

1. In a Web browser, go to the URL of your group (such as http://groups.mac. com/*groupname*, replacing *groupname* with your group's short name).

   You'll be presented with the login page (see Figure 7.2).

2. Enter your member name and password, and click Login.

   Your group's home page is loaded (**Figure 7.30**).

   continues on next page

Figure 7.29 If you're invited to a .Mac group, simply click the "Join group now" link in the invitation e-mail to accept.

Figure 7.30 The first step to managing members of your group is to load your main group page.

Accepting an Invitation *(continued)*

Figure 7.31 The "Manage group membership" page lets you search for members, e-mail or remove members, invite new members, approve pending invitations, and view any invitations that you've sent.

Figure 7.32 Click "Back to group" to return to your group page after managing the members of the group.

3. In the Members section of the sidebar on the left, click the Manage link.

   The group's membership page loads, showing members, invitations, and any pending approvals (**Figure 7.31**).

4. On this page, *do one of the following:*

   ▲ To invite a new member, click the Invite button in the upper right corner, and then follow the on-screen instructions for inviting someone (see Steps 4-8 of "To invite others to your group").

   ▲ To cancel a pending invitation, check the box to the left of the invitation to cancel, and click Cancel Invitation.

   ▲ To approve a pending invitation (referred from someone else), check the box to the left of the invitation to approve and click Approve Invitation (which only appears if there are any pending invitations to approve).

5. When finished, click the "Back to group" button (**Figure 7.32**). The group's page loads.

✔ Tip

■ To find a group member's profile, enter the member's name in the search field, and click the magnifying glass icon to search.

Editing an Existing Group

After you create a group, you may want to make a few changes to it. Fortunately, you can quickly edit your group's settings with a few clicks.

To edit an existing group:

1. Log in to your .Mac account following steps 1–3 of "To create a group."

   The list of groups you've created and that you belong to is listed.

2. Click the Groups link in the navigation bar.

   Your groups page loads, listing any groups that you have already set up (**Figure 7.33**).

3. Just below the group title, click the Edit link.

   The Edit Group page loads (**Figure 7.34**).

4. Make any changes you want to elements of your group, including the name, description, time zone, or color scheme, and then click Save.

   You are returned to the group list, and your changes have been saved.

✔ Tip

■ You can adjust how much of your iDisk space is reserved for your group by visiting the Storage Settings page for your .Mac account.

Figure 7.33 Any groups that you have already created are listed on your main Groups page.

Figure 7.34 On the Edit Group page, you can make changes to your group's setup.

Figure 7.35 Your group homepage shows no messages, yet—you (or another member) need to add them.

To post a message to your group:

1. In a Web browser, go to the URL of your group (such as http://groups.mac.com/ *groupname*, replacing *groupname* with your group's short name).

   You'll be presented with the login page (see Figure 7.2).

2. Enter your member name and password, and click Login.

   Your group's home page is loaded (**Figure 7.35**).

3. Click the Compose link in the Messages section.

   The "Compose a message" page loads (**Figure 7.36**).

   continues on next page

Figure 7.36 The "Compose a message" page lets you create and post a message to your site—and send it to your group members.

EDITING AN EXISTING GROUP

4. In the fields, *do the following:*

   ▲ In the Cc field, type any additional e-mail addresses you want the message to go to.

   ▲ In the main text area, type your message.

   ▲ Click the "Spell check" button to check your message for spelling errors.

5. To attach a file, *do the following:*

   ▲ Click the Attach button.

   ▲ On the next page, click the Choose File button.

   ▲ Navigate to the file you want to attach in the file-selection dialog that opens, and click Choose.

   ▲ Click the "Attach and done" button. Your file appears in the Attachments section (**Figure 7.37**).

6. Click Send.

Your message is sent, and a page appears, notifying you of that (**Figure 7.38**).

7. Click "Get messages" to reload your message list.

Your new message appears in the list (**Figure 7.39**). It also appears on the main group page.

✔ Tips

■ To send a message to your group e-mail address, address it to the e-mail address you set up when you created the group. The message will be e-mailed to all members.

■ To delete a message, click the message's title, and then click the Delete button. The message will be removed.

Figure 7.37 After you've uploaded a file to your message, its name appears in the Attachments section of the composition window.

Figure 7.38 The group messages page reloads, and it displays a line of text at the top, reading, "Your message was sent."

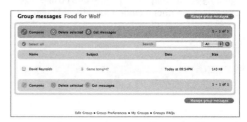

Figure 7.39 After you refresh your messages via the "Get messages" button, your new message appears in the list.

■ To reply to a message, click the message's title, and when the next page loads, check the box next to the message you want to reply to, click the Reply button, type your reply, and click Send. Off you go . . .

Publishing a Group Calendar

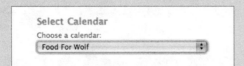

Figure 7.40 Choose the iCal calendar you want associated with your group from the Select Calendar pop-up menu.

You can use iCal to post calendar events to your group's page by publishing a calendar to your .Mac account. Here's how.

Create a calendar for your group, and publish it to your .Mac account. (For complete information on using iCal with your .Mac account, see Chapter 11, "Using iCal.")

Load the Edit page for your group, and in the Select Calendar section choose the calendar you want to use from the pop-up menu (**Figure 7.40**); click Save.

When you visit the homepage, your calendar events will show up on the group calendar. A date with an event will be blue, and if you click it, the calendar's day will load in a new window (**Figure 7.41**). Simple, huh? Users can even subscribe to the group calendar with iCal from this page.

Figure 7.41 When you click a day on the group calendar, a new page loads, listing all of the events for that day for your group.

To access the group iDisk:

1. In a Web browser, go to the URL of your group (such as http://groups.mac.com/ *groupname*, replacing *groupname* with your group's short name).

   You'll be presented with the login page (see Figure 7.2).

2. Enter your member name and password, and click Login.

   Your group's home page is loaded (see Figure 7.30).

3. On the left side of the page, click the globe button to the right of the Group iDisk label.

   A new browser window opens with a login dialog (**Figure 7.42**).

4. Enter your member name and password, and click Log In.

   Your group's iDisk page is loaded (**Figure 7.43**).

You can use the group's iDisk as you would your normal iDisk. See "Connecting to Your iDisk with a Browser" in Chapter 3, "Using iDisk," for complete details.

Figure 7.42 To access your group's iDisk, you'll need to enter your .Mac member name and password, and then click Log In.

Figure 7.43 Your group iDisk page is an ideal place to share movies, pictures, or other files.

Figure 7.44 The Other Links controls let you enter a new link by typing a name and URL, and then clicking Add.

Figure 7.45 After entering a name and URL for the link to be added, click the Add button.

Figure 7.46 After you add a link, it appears in the Other Links section of your Group home-page, and an Edit link replaces "Add a link."

✔ Tip

■ The Edit link is used just like "Add a link" for placing additional links on your Group homepage, but it also gives you the option of removing any custom link by checking a box next to its name and clicking Delete (**Figure 7.47**).

To add a link to the page:

1. In a Web browser, go to the URL of your group (such as http://groups.mac.com/ *groupname*, replacing *groupname* with your group's short name).

   You'll be presented with the login page (see Figure 7.2).

2. Enter your member name and password, and click Login.

   Your group's home page is loaded (see Figure 7.30).

3. In the lower left corner of the page, click the "Add a link" link.

   The link expands into an area that allows you to enter a link name and URL (**Figure 7.44**).

4. In the Link Name field, enter a name for the link, and in the Link URL field, enter the site's URL; then click Add (**Figure 7.45**).

   The link shows up in the Other Links section, and the "Add a link" link changes to one that reads "Edit" (**Figure 7.46**).

Figure 7.47 To remove a custom link from the Other Links section of your Group homepage, click the Edit link, check the box next to the name of the link to be removed, and click Delete.

Calling It Quits

The day may come, after you've set up and nurtured a lively .Mac group, when you feel it's time to turn management duties over to another member of the community. Or you may choose to shut down a group once its reason to exist (planning an event, for example) has gone. In either case, .Mac Group Preferences is the key to a smooth transition.

To transfer group ownership:

1. Log in to your .Mac account following steps 1–3 of "To create a group."

   The list of groups you've created and that you belong to is listed.

2. Click the Groups link in the navigation bar.

   Your "My groups" page loads, listing all groups that you own or have joined (see Figure 7.33).

3. Click the Group Preferences link at the bottom of the page.

   The "Group preferences" page loads (**Figure 7.48**).

4. Click the "Transfer ownership" link to the right of the name of the group you want to transfer.

   A list of all group members with full .Mac membership accounts appears.

5. Click the radio button to the left of your successor's name, and then click the Send button.

✔ Tip

- If the "Group preferences" page doesn't show a "Transfer ownership" link next to the name of a group you own, that means no other member of that group has a paid .Mac subscription. Only paying subscribers can own groups, so you'll have to get someone to pony up before you can hand over the reins.

Figure 7.48 To delete a group or transfer ownership to another group member, use the "Group preferences" page.

Figure 7.49 Before you delete a page, you are warned that clicking the Yes button will remove the group, delete its files, and cause all of its messages to bounce.

Figure 7.50 Once you've clicked Yes, a page loads, telling you that the group has been deleted.

To delete a group:

1. Follow steps 1–3 of "To transfer group ownership" to display your "Group preferences" page (see Figure 7.48).

2. Click the "Cancel group" link to the right of the name of the group you want to delete.

   The cancellation-confirmation page loads, warning you that the group will be canceled, messages to it will bounce, and pages published to it will be lost (**Figure 7.49**).

3. Click Yes.

   The group is deleted (**Figure 7.50**).

USING .MAC SYNC

Your .Mac account doesn't just provide a great ad-free e-mail address, online storage, and the ability to whip up Web pages in a flash. It also serves as a repository for your personal information—your Safari bookmarks, Address Book contacts, iCal calendars, Mail accounts and rules, and Mac OS X keychains (which hold encrypted passwords for various accounts).

There are two great things about this: The first is that storing this information on your .Mac account lets you transfer it easily to any other Macintosh computer. Copying the items to another Mac is as easy as logging in to your .Mac account from that computer and clicking a button. The second great thing about storing personal information on .Mac is that you can access most of this information (such as your contacts and Safari bookmarks) from just about any computer with a Web browser and an Internet connection. With a little cleverness, you can even copy your information to a cell phone, iPod, or Palm PDA.

Five software tools allow you to do this. You'll need your .Mac account, iSync, Address Book, Safari, and iCal. All of these come with the latest version of Mac OS X, and they can be downloaded from Apple for older versions of Mac OS X. A sixth important tool—.Mac Sync—is built right into Mac OS X v10.4 Tiger.

In this chapter, I'll show you how to set up Mac OS X 10.4's .Mac Sync, how to use it to synchronize information between two (or more) Macs using your .Mac account, and how to use iSync to integrate other devices in your synchronization routine.

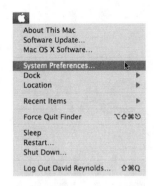

Figure 8.1 Choose System Preferences from the Apple menu to open the application.

Figure 8.2 Click the .Mac icon to load the .Mac preferences.

Figure 8.3 The .Mac pane opens, by default, to the Account tab.

Setting Up .Mac Sync

With the advent of Mac OS X v10.4, Apple integrated something called .Mac Sync into the operating system. This simply means that Mac OS X knows how to talk to your .Mac account directly and how to share your important information with it. To enable your Mac to do that, you first have to set up the .Mac System Preferences to work appropriately. Note that your computer will need to be connected to the Internet in order for Sync setup to work correctly.

To set up .Mac Sync:

1. From the Apple menu, choose System Preferences (**Figure 8.1**).

   System Preferences launches, and the main System Preferences window opens.

2. Click the .Mac icon in the Internet & Network section (**Figure 8.2**).

   The .Mac pane opens, with the Account tab selected by default (**Figure 8.3**).

3. If you haven't done so previously, enter your .Mac member name and password in the appropriate fields.

continues on next page

SETTING UP .MAC SYNC

4. Click the Sync tab.

The .Mac Sync preferences load (**Figure 8.4**).

5. At the top of the pane, check the Synchronize with .Mac box. This turns .Mac synchronization on.

6. From the Synchronize with .Mac pop-up menu, choose whether you want synchronizations to take place manually (only when you tell the computer to sync your account) or automatically. If automatically, you should also choose how frequently you want updates to occur (hourly, daily, or weekly) (**Figure 8.5**).

7. Check the boxes next to the items you want synchronized. Your choices are Bookmarks, Calendars, Contacts, Keychains, Mail Accounts, and Mail Rules, Signatures, and Smart Mailboxes (for a rundown on each of these, see the sidebar "What .Mac Sync Synchronizes").

8. If you want to have the Sync icon appear in the menu bar, check the "Show status in menu bar" box at the bottom of the window.

9. From the System Preferences application menu, choose Quit System Preferences (Command-Q) to quit the application and save your .Mac Sync changes (**Figure 8.6**).

✔ Tip

■ Whether you choose automatic or manual syncing, you can perform a manual synchronization anytime by clicking the Sync Now button at the bottom of the .Mac Sync preferences pane.

Figure 8.4 Clicking the Sync tab opens the .Mac Sync preferences, where you can control what is synchronized, and when.

Figure 8.5 From the pop-up menu, you can choose whether synchronizations happen automatically (hourly, daily, or weekly) or manually.

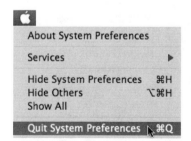

Figure 8.6 From the System Preferences applications menu, choose Quit System Preferences to quit the application and save your changes.

Figure 8.7 Clicking the Sync Now button causes a synchronization to happen immediately.

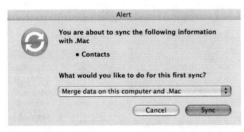

Figure 8.8 The first time you perform a synchronization, an alert pops up asking you how you want to handle the data transfer.

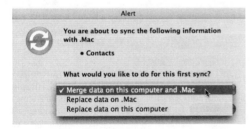

Figure 8.9 From the pop-up menu, choose whether you'd like to merge data or replace it in one place or another.

Performing Your First Sync

The first time you synchronize your computer to your .Mac account is different from other synchronizations. Before your first sync, you must make some choices about how things will proceed during the synchronization. Mainly, you have to decide whether information will be *merged* or *replaced*.

In a merge synchronization, the information stored on your computer is combined with any information stored on your .Mac account (such as information copied from another computer or from an earlier synchronization of the computer you're currently using). In a replacement synchronization, all the information on one side of the transfer (your computer or the .Mac account) is erased and replaced by a copy of the information stored on the other side. If you choose to do a replacement synchronization, you must therefore specify which set of information will be kept and copied, and which will be discarded.

To perform your first sync:

1. In the .Mac Sync System Preferences pane, set up a sync and click Sync Now (**Figure 8.7**).

   An alert dialog opens, asking what you would like to do for this first sync (**Figure 8.8**).

2. From the pop-up menu, *choose one of the following* (**Figure 8.9**):

   ▲ **"Merge data on this computer and .Mac."** This choice, selected by default, does its best to consolidate the information on your Mac with that in your .Mac account, leaving the sum total of all information on both sides of the transfer.

   continues on next page

▲ **"Replace data on .Mac."** This choice replaces the information in your .Mac account with the information on your Mac. Choose this when you want the information on your computer be the starting point for all synchronizations—or if there is no information in your .Mac account in the first place. Remember: Choosing this option will erase all of the synchronized information in your .Mac account for the category listed in the dialog.

▲ **"Replace data on this computer."** This choice replaces the information on your Mac with the information in your .Mac account. Choose this when you want to use the information in your .Mac account as the starting point for all synchronizations. This is especially useful when you want to set up a new computer with your .Mac data without having to reenter contact information, Safari bookmarks, or Mail accounts.

3. Click Sync.

Your Mac begins synchronizing its information with your .Mac account. If you're merging information and there is conflicting data, the Conflict Resolver dialog opens, and you're given the choice of reviewing information now or later (**Figure 8.10**). The dialog also tells you how many data points conflict, so that you have some idea what you may be getting into if you choose Review Now.

4. Click Review Now.

The Conflict Resolver dialog expands to show the "Select the correct information" section, where the two pieces of conflicting information appear side by side (**Figure 8.11**).

Figure 8.10 If you're synchronizing conflicting information when merging data—such as two contacts with the same name but different addresses—the Conflict Resolver dialog appears.

Figure 8.11 When you have to choose between two conflicting bits of data, the choice is presented clearly in the Conflict Resolver dialog. Simply click the side with the correct information.

PERFORMING YOUR FIRST SYNC

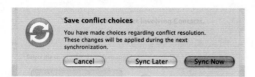

Figure 8.12 After you've made your selection in each conflict, the "Save conflict choices" dialog opens, asking you to synchronize your information again. Click the Sync Now button to perform another sync.

5. Click the side with the correct information to resolve the conflict.

If there is more than one conflict, the next one loads in the dialog. Choose the correct information for each by clicking the proper side. When you've gone through all of the conflicts, the "Save conflict choices" dialog appears, noting that the changes will be applied the next time you perform a synchronization (**Figure 8.12**).

6. Click Sync Now.

Your Mac synchronizes its information with your .Mac account, resolving the conflicts as you directed.

✔ Tips

■ If you want to investigate the Conflict Resolver, you can induce a conflict by synchronizing your data, making two separate edits to one of your contacts; and then resynchronizing.

■ If you have more than one conflict to resolve, a checkbox appears allowing you to apply the same rule to all conflicts — specifying that the local versions of all contacts should be used instead of those on the server, for instance, or vice-versa. You can also review each conflict separately and decide which to use on a case-by-case basis.

■ When you perform a .Mac synchronization for the first time, you may be shown the "first sync" alert dialog a few times— asking you to specify different rules for handling Address Book contacts, Mail accounts, iCal calendars, and so on.

■ If you see the Conflict Resolver dialog open, don't panic—it often means minor adjustments. Conflicting information can be as major as entirely different phone numbers and addresses for a given contact, or it can be as simple as having different user images associated with an account.

Manual Synchronization

If you've set up your .Mac Sync preferences to Automatic, Every Hour, Every Day, or Every Week, your computer will automatically synchronize your data on the schedule you've set. If you've set it to Manually, however, you'll have to be the one to initiate a sync.

To perform a manual sync:

1. From the Apple menu, choose System Preferences.

   The System Preferences application launches, and the main System Preferences window opens.

2. Click the .Mac icon.

   The .Mac pane opens, with the Account tab selected.

3. Click the Sync tab.

   The .Mac Sync preferences load.

4. In the lower right corner of the .Mac Sync preferences, click the Sync Now button (**Figure 8.13**).

   Your Mac synchronizes your information with your .Mac account.

✔ Tip

■ If you've checked the "Show status in menu bar" box, you can choose Sync Now from the Sync menu to initiate a sync (**Figure 8.14**).

Figure 8.13 Clicking the Sync Now button causes a synchronization to happen immediately.

Figure 8.14 If you elected to have Sync in the menu bar, you can perform a synchronization at any time by selecting Sync Now from that menu.

What .Mac Sync Synchronizes

You may be curious about what each of those check boxes in the .Mac Sync preferences represents. After all, it's good to know what information gets synchronized to your .Mac account. Here's a rundown:

◆ **Bookmarks**—Your Safari bookmarks

◆ **Calendars**—Your iCal calendars

◆ **Contacts**—Your Address Book contact information

◆ **Keychains**—Your Keychain-managed login information (including passwords)

◆ **Mail Accounts**—Your Mail account information for all accounts

◆ **Mail Rules, Signatures, and Smart Mailboxes**—Rules, signatures, and any Smart Mailboxes that you've set up

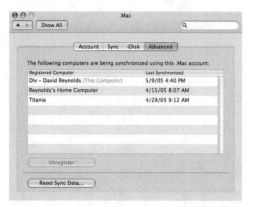

Figure 8.15 The Advanced pane lets you control which computers are authorized to synchronize with your .Mac account, as well as reset synchronization data.

Figure 8.16 Before you're allowed to unregister a computer, a dialog slides down to ask if you're sure— and to warn you of the consequences (which are minor). Click Unregister.

Unregistering a Mac

When you perform a synchronization to your .Mac account, any Mac you use to initiate a sync is automatically registered with your .Mac account. If you sell your Mac or otherwise don't want a computer associated with your .Mac account (for example, if you sync a temporary user account set up on a friend's computer), you can unregister the computer from your .Mac account so that it's no longer eligible for synchronization.

To unregister a Mac:

1. From the Apple menu, choose System Preferences.

   The System Preferences application launches, and the main System Preferences window opens.

2. Click the .Mac icon.

   The .Mac pane opens, with the Account tab selected.

3. Click the Advanced tab.

   The .Mac Advanced preferences load, showing all computers registered for synchronization with your .Mac account (**Figure 8.15**).

4. From the Registered Computer list, select the computer that you want to unregister, and click the Unregister button.

   A dialog slides down, asking if you're sure that you want to unregister the selected computer (**Figure 8.16**).

continues on next page

5. Click Unregister.

After a short wait, the selected computer is unregistered and no longer appears in the list (**Figure 8.17**).

6. From the System Preferences application menu, choose Quit System Preferences (Command-Q) to quit the application and save your .Mac Sync changes.

System Preferences quits.

✔ Tip

■ Unregistering doesn't require logging in to your .Mac account from the computer you want to unregister. You can do it from any Macintosh. If the Mac you're using isn't registered to your .Mac account, you'll have to register it temporarily, and then just select it along with the Mac you originally wanted to unregister, and unregister them both.

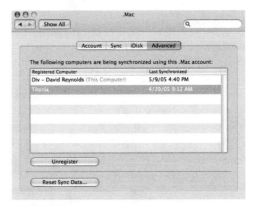

Figure 8.17 After you unregister a computer, it no longer appears in the Registered Computer list.

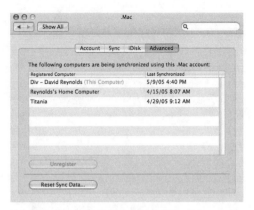

Figure 8.18 The Reset Sync Data button allows you to "take back" the last synchronization you've done, by replacing the synchronized data with a copy.

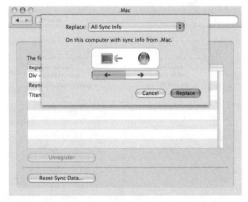

Figure 8.19 When you click the Reset Sync Data button, a dialog slides down, presenting you with some options on what data to replace and where.

Resetting Sync Data

Anytime your computer is connected to the Internet, you can reset your .Mac Sync data— a process that's essentially the same as using the replacement synchronization option presented the first time you sync a computer with .Mac. Resetting your data either replaces all the data on your computer with information stored on your .Mac account, or vice versa. It's a useful option if you accidentally delete some critical information on your Macintosh, botch an import into your Address Book, or just decide you want to undo changes made on .Mac during your last sync.

To reset your sync data:

1. From the Apple menu, choose System Preferences.

   The System Preferences application launches, and the main System Preferences window opens.

2. Click the .Mac icon.

   The .Mac pane opens, with the Account tab selected.

3. Click the Advanced tab.

   The .Mac Advanced preferences load, showing all computers registered to be synchronized with your .Mac account.

4. Click the Reset Sync Data button (**Figure 8.18**).

   A dialog slides down, asking for specifics on which information to reset and what to use as the replacement source, indicated by two arrows (**Figure 8.19**).

   continues on next page

5. From the Replace pop-up menu at the top of the dialog, *choose one of the following to reset* (**Figure 8.20**):

▲ **All Sync Info.** This replaces all information.

▲ **Bookmarks.** This replaces just your Safari bookmarks.

▲ **Calendars.** This replaces just your calendar information.

▲ **Contacts.** This replaces just your contact information.

▲ **Keychains.** This replaces just your keychain information.

▲ **Mail Accounts.** This replaces just your Mail account information.

▲ **Mail Rules, Signatures, and Smart Mailboxes.** This replaces just the Mail rules, signatures, and any Smart Mailboxes (mailboxes created using a Spotlight search) you've created.

6. Click one of the arrow buttons to choose whether information is to be replaced on the computer or on the .Mac account.

Clicking the left arrow replaces information on the computer with information from the .Mac account. Clicking the right arrow replaces information on the .Mac account with information from the computer.

7. Click Replace.

The information is replaced as specified during the next synchronization.

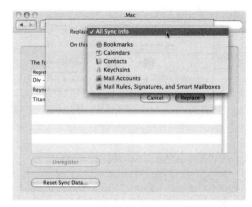

Figure 8.20 The Replace pop-up menu allows you to choose which data you want to replace—including replacing all data.

RESETTING SYNC DATA

Figure 8.21 The iSync window starts out with just one icon—the one labeled .mac.

Figure 8.22 To add a device to iSync, choose Devices > Add Device or press Command-N.

Figure 8.23 When an eligible device is found, the Add Device window expands to provide details. In this case, iSync has discovered a V60 cell phone connected by USB.

Syncing a Phone, PDA, or iPod

Mac OS X v10.4 comes with a utility program called iSync, which lets you synchronize some of your information to handheld devices—such as cell phones, iPods, and PDAs—in addition to your .Mac account.

To use iSync with a handheld device:

1. Connect your phone, PDA, or iPod to your Mac via its USB cable; or, if your phone or PDA supports it, use a Bluetooth wireless connection. (You may need to consult your device's manual for guidance on this.)

2. In the Applications folder, double-click iSync to launch it.

   The iSync window opens (**Figure 8.21**). By default, it has one lonely little icon representing devices it can sync with—the icon for your .Mac account. (The account isn't really a "device," of course, but iSync treats it as one.)

3. From the Devices menu, choose Add Device (Command-N) (**Figure 8.22**).

   The Add Device window opens, and iSync scans for any eligible connected devices. When it finds your phone, iPod, or PDA, it notifies you in the Add Device window (**Figure 8.23**).

continues on next page

4. Double-click the found device to add it to iSync.

iSync adds the device and displays its preferences (**Figure 8.24**). The preferences in this window vary according to the specific type and model of device you've connected.

5. From the "For first sync" pop-up menu, *choose one of the following:*

▲ "Merge data on computer and device" to preserve data on both the phone and your Mac, merging it and reporting any conflicting data to you

▲ "Erase data on device then sync" to erase the phone data and replace its data with information from your Mac

6. Check the "Turn on *device name* synchronization" box.

This ensures that data on the device will be synchronized.

7. Check the boxes next to the information you want synchronized. This varies depending on the device, but it can include contact information, calendar events, and to-do items.

8. In the upper right corner of the iSync window, click the Sync Devices button.

iSync synchronizes information between your phone, your Mac, and your .Mac account (**Figure 8.25**).

Figure 8.24 After a device has been added, its preferences are displayed. These preferences differ, based on the kind and model of device detected.

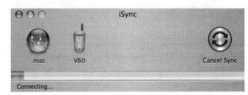

Figure 8.25 iSync presents a progress bar when information is being synchronized between your computer, a device, and your .Mac account.

✔ Tips

- Not all cell phones work with iSync. To check your phone's compatibility, visit Apple's "iSync Compatible Devices" page (www.apple.com/macosx/features/isync/devices.html). Note that you may need to purchase a data cable separately.

- If you're using a Bluetooth phone, be sure it has been set up using the Bluetooth preferences pane in System Preferences before you set up iSync to work with it. (If you don't see a Bluetooth icon in the main System Preferences window, your Mac doesn't have a Bluetooth module installed.)

- The .Mac icon in iSync 2.0 doesn't do much—it presents a dialog noting that you have to change your .Mac Sync preferences in the .Mac pane of System Preferences. That dialog has a button called Open .Mac Preferences, which, if clicked, opens the .Mac pane of System Preferences.

- iSync synchronizes data stored on your phone with the records in the Address Book and iCal applications installed on the Macintosh you're synchronizing with—not with the data stored on your .Mac account. It's a good idea to do a .Mac sync, to make sure that Address Book and iCal are fully up-to-date, before you sync a phone or other device using iSync.

iSync for Mac OS X v10.2 or v10.3

Mac OS X v10.2 Jaguar and v10.3 Panther do not have built-in .Mac synchronization capabilities, but if you don't have Mac OS X v10.4, don't despair. You can download a version of iSync that works with Mac OS X v10.2 and v10.3.

This version of iSync (version 1.5) works with some cell phones and iPods, and it also controls how your Mac synchronizes its information with your .Mac account. With iSync 1.5, all synchronization is done with iSync.

You can download iSync 1.5 from the Apple Web site at www.apple.com/support/downloads/isync.html.

SYNCING A PHONE, PDA, OR IPOD

Removing a Device from iSync

iSync allows you to remove a device you previously added, so that it's no longer synchronized—say, you give your iPod to your kid or you upgrade your cell phone and need to remove the old one.

To remove a device from iSync:

1. In the Applications folder, double-click iSync to launch it.

   The iSync window opens (**Figure 8.26**).

2. Click the icon of the device you want to remove.

   The window expands to show the device's preferences (**Figure 8.27**).

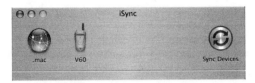

Figure 8.26 When iSync is launched after a device is added, the device's icon appears in the main iSync window.

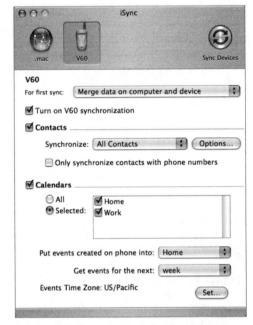

Figure 8.27 Before a device can be removed from iSync, you must select its icon, which expands the window to reveal the iSync preferences for the device.

Figure 8.28 To remove a device, choose Remove Device from the Devices menu.

Figure 8.29 Before you're allowed to remove a device from iSync, you're asked to confirm the action. Click OK.

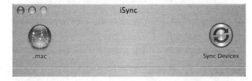

Figure 8.30 After the device is removed, the iSync window returns to its previous size—minus the removed device's icon.

3. From the Devices menu, choose Remove Device (**Figure 8.28**).

   A dialog opens asking if you want to remove the device from iSync (**Figure 8.29**).

4. Click OK.

   The device is removed from iSync (**Figure 8.30**).

Setting .Mac iSync Preferences

iSync has a number of preferences you can tweak to control how your computer, your .Mac account, and any devices that you've set up share information (**Figure 8.31**). To access the iSync Preferences, choose Preferences from the iSync menu.

Here's what each preference does:

◆ **"Enable syncing on this computer."** With this check box you turn synchronization on and off for this computer, as well as for your .Mac account.

◆ **"Show HotSync reminder when syncing Palm OS devices."** If you're using a Palm OS–based device, with this check box you tell iSync to show the HotSync reminder when you use iSync with it.

◆ **"Show status in menu bar."** This check box allows you to have the Sync menu appear in the menu bar.

◆ **"Show Data Change Alert when."** This pop-up menu lets you set how much of your personal information can be changed before an alert pops up. By default, an alert appears if more than 5 percent of the data on your computer changes during a synchronization (**Figure 8.32**).

◆ **Reset Sync History.** You click this button to reset the Mac's synchronization history, which effectively wipes the slate clean. After you reset your sync history, the computer behaves as if it were the first time a synchronization had taken place. See the section "Performing Your First Sync" for more on what happens during a first synchronization.

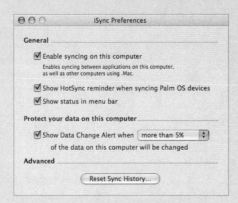

Figure 8.31 iSync's preferences allow you some control over how iSync behaves.

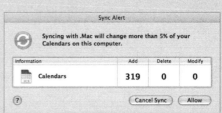

Figure 8.32 If more than a certain amount of information will be changed by a synchronization, an alert dialog provides some details on what's happening—including what's being changed; how many items are being added, deleted, or modified; and whether the synchronization should be allowed or canceled.

USING ADDRESS BOOK

In Chapter 8, "Using .Mac Sync," we covered how to turn on .Mac Sync to synchronize your Safari bookmarks, iCal calendars, Address Book contacts, Mac OS X keychains, and Mail accounts to your .Mac account. Once you've done that, you're ready to start tapping into one of .Mac's most powerful features: the ability to access all of that luscious contact information from anywhere in the world using a Web browser and an Internet connection.

After you've performed a synchronization, you can look up contact information in your .Mac Address Book from any computer, and you can also use those contacts to quickly address e-mail messages from within .Mac's Webmail interface.

In this chapter, I'll show you how to set Address Book preferences, add and remove contacts from Address Book, and browse and search through the contact information stored in your .Mac Address Book using a Web browser. I'll also explain how to edit contacts and share the contact information stored in your Mac OS X 10.4 Tiger Address Book with others.

An important note: In this chapter, we're talking about two separate things that are both named *Address Book*. Your Mac OS X Address Book is an application that lets you store and organize contact information; your .Mac Address Book is an area of your .Mac account that stores contact information. Through Mac OS X synchronization, you can keep the information in your Mac OS X Address Book and .Mac Address Book identical.

Setting .Mac Address Book Preferences

Your .Mac Address Book allows you to set some preferences that govern how it behaves. By changing these preferences, you can select the number of contacts displayed per page, change how addresses are sorted, choose the defaults for the kind of data you enter, and turn on (or off) Address Book Synchronization.

To set .Mac Address Book preferences:

1. At www.mac.com, log in to your .Mac account.

   The main .Mac welcome page opens, with you logged in (**Figure 9.1**).

2. Click the Address Book link at the top of the page or in the column on the left.

   The main .Mac Address Book page opens, listing your contacts and their e-mail addresses and phone numbers (**Figure 9.2**).

Figure 9.1 After you've logged in to your .Mac account, your .Mac member name appears in the upper right corner of the page.

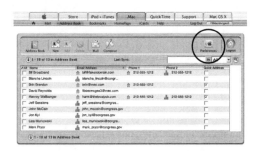

Figure 9.2 When you open your .Mac Address Book, the contacts are listed in groups of ten, and a toolbar appears at the top of the page. Click the Preferences button to open the Preferences page.

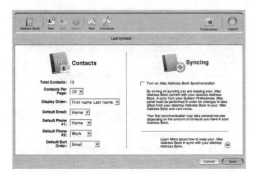

Figure 9.3 The .Mac Address Book Preferences page lets you set how your .Mac Address Book behaves.

3. Click the Preferences button at the top of the .Mac Address Book page.

   The .Mac Address Book Preferences page opens (**Figure 9.3**). On this page, you can see how many contacts are in your .Mac Address Book, and you can set how it behaves.

4. On the .Mac Address Book preferences page, *do the following:*

   ▲ Select the number of contacts to be displayed per page from the Contacts Per Page pop-up menu.

   ▲ Select whether addresses are sorted by last name or first name from the Display Order pop-up menu.

   ▲ Choose whether Home or Work is set as the default e-mail address in the Default Email pop-up menu.

   ▲ Choose whether Home, Work, Mobile, or Fax is set as the default phone number in the Default Phone #1 pop-up menu.

   ▲ Choose whether Home, Work, Mobile, or Fax is set as the default phone number in the Default Phone #2 pop-up menu.

   ▲ Choose whether Email, Last Name, or First Name is set as the default sort order in the Default Sort Order pop-up menu.

   ▲ Check the Turn on .Mac Address Book Synchronization box to turn on Address Book synchronization (as covered in Chapter 8).

5. Click Save.

   Your preferences are saved, and the main Address Book page opens.

✔ **Tip**

■ You can go right to your .Mac Address Book by pointing your Web browser to http://addressbook.mac.com (there's no *www*). If this is the first time you've accessed your Address Book via .Mac and you've already performed a sync, you may be told that you'll have to perform an additional sync—this time from your .Mac account to your computer.

Adding Contacts to Address Book

.Mac does a fabulous job of pulling updated information from your local Address Book application that comes with Mac OS X through .Mac Sync (as described in Chapter 8). It's not the only way to add contact information to your .Mac account, though. You can also add contacts using your Web browser.

To add a contact using a Web browser:

1. Log in to your .Mac Address Book.

   The main .Mac Address Book page opens (**Figure 9.4**).

2. In the toolbar at the top of the page, click the New button.

   The new-contact page opens (**Figure 9.5**).

3. In the fields on the new-contact page, enter as much of the following information as you like:

   ▲ Personal information, such as first name, last name, title, and company

   ▲ Physical addresses for work and home

   ▲ E-mail addresses for work and home

   ▲ AIM account information for work and home

   ▲ Telephone numbers for work, home, mobile phone, and fax

   ▲ URL for the contact's homepage

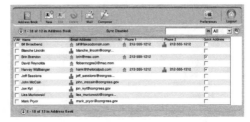

Figure 9.4 The .Mac Web Address Book also lists contacts in groups of ten, and it provides a toolbar with some common commands.

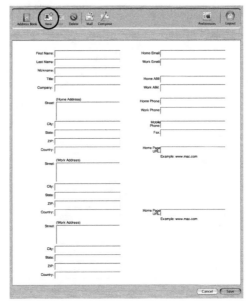

Figure 9.5 When you click the New button in the toolbar, the new-contact page opens. On it, you can enter as much contact information as you like.

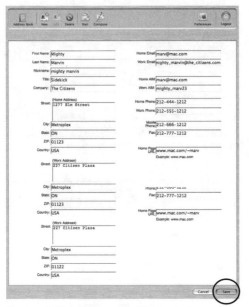

Figure 9.6 After you've entered the contact information, click Save.

4. Click Save (**Figure 9.6**).

You are returned to the main .Mac Address Book page. The new contact shows in the contact list (**Figure 9.7**). The next time you sync your computer(s) with your .Mac account, the new contact information will also be copied to your computer's Mac OS X Address Book application. If you add a contact and immediately synchronize, however, you may not see the changes right away. Wait a few minutes and try synchronizing again.

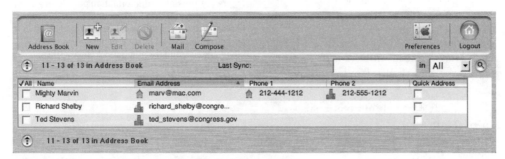

Figure 9.7 The new contact appears in your .Mac Address Book.

Viewing Contact Information

When you log in to your .Mac Address Book at www.mac.com, a page opens displaying a list of your contacts. If you don't have a lot of contacts, you might just want to browse through the list until you find the person you need to reach. When your contacts start getting more numerous, however, performing a search for the person you need to get in touch with will save you time.

To browse contact information:

1. Log in to your .Mac Address Book.

   The main .Mac Address Book page opens, listing your contacts and their e-mail addresses and phone numbers.

2. In the lower left corner of the page, click the downward-pointing arrow to bring up the next set of ten addresses (**Figure 9.8**).

   The next set of ten addresses appears.

3. Click a name, e-mail address, or phone number to bring up the detailed information for that contact.

   The contact's detailed-information page opens (**Figure 9.9**).

✔ Tip

■ You can also browse backward through your addresses, ten at a time, by clicking the upward-pointing arrow at the bottom of the Address Book window. (This assumes you're not viewing the first page of addresses, from which it's impossible to go backward.)

Figure 9.8 To see the next set of ten contacts, click the downward-pointing arrow.

Figure 9.9 The detailed-information page for a given contact contains only as much information as you've entered, but it *can* include name; work and home addresses; work and home e-mail addresses; work, home, mobile, and fax numbers; Web-site URLs, and more.

Figure 9.10 If you want to restrict your search to just names, e-mail addresses, or phone numbers, you can do so by selecting the appropriate filter from the "in" pop-up menu.

Figure 9.11 Once the search is complete, its results are displayed in a list.

To search contact information:

1. Log in to your .Mac Address Book.

   The main .Mac Address Book page opens.

2. In the upper right corner of the Address Book page, type your search term. It can be a name, an e-mail address, or a phone number.

3. From the "in" pop-up menu, choose the criterion you want to use to restrict your search (if you want to use any). The default choice is All; you can restrict your search to names, e-mail addresses, or phone numbers (**Figure 9.10**).

4. Click the magnifying glass button to conduct the search.

   The search results page appears, showing you all the matches (**Figure 9.11**).

VIEWING CONTACT INFORMATION

Editing Contact Information

At times, you may need to change a contact's information—say you've misspelled an e-mail address, you need to use it for a series of messages, and you don't feel much like correcting it every time.

Figure 9.12 Check the box to the left of the address you want to edit.

To edit contact information:

1. Log in to your .Mac Address Book.

   The main .Mac Address Book page opens.

2. Check the box to the left of the contact you want to edit (**Figure 9.12**). You can edit only one contact at a time.

3. At the top of the page, click the Edit button.

   The contact-editing page opens (**Figure 9.13**).

4. Make any necessary changes to the contact's information, and click Save.

   Your changes are saved, and the main .Mac Address Book page opens.

Figure 9.13 On the contact-editing page, you can make any changes you like to the selected contact's information.

Figure 9.14 Check the boxes next to the contacts you want to delete.

Figure 9.15 Before any contacts are deleted, you are asked if you want to go through with the deletion. Click Yes to continue.

To delete a contact:

1. Log in to your .Mac Address Book.

   The main .Mac Address Book page opens.

2. Check the boxes to the left of all the contacts you want to delete (**Figure 9.14**). You can delete more than one contact at a time.

3. Click the Delete button.

   A page appears, asking if you're sure you want to delete the selected contacts (**Figure 9.15**).

4. If you're sure you want to delete the contacts, click Yes.

   The selected contacts are deleted, and the main Address Book page opens.

Sharing Address Book Information

Mac OS X 10.4 has an updated version of Address Book with one great new feature: Address Book sharing. With this feature, you can share your Address Book contacts with anyone listed in your Address Book application who has a .Mac account, and you can choose whether those people can edit your contacts or just read them. Likewise, if another .Mac member has included you (using your .Mac e-mail address) in his or her list of authorized Address Book sharers, you can subscribe to that person's information using Address Book.

To share your Address Book information:

1. In the Applications folder, double-click the Address Book icon to open the application.

   The main Address Book window opens (**Figure 9.16**).

2. From the Address Book menu, choose Preferences (**Figure 9.17**).

   The Address Book Preferences window opens to the General pane by default (**Figure 9.18**).

Figure 9.16 The first step to sharing an Address Book is to open the Address Book application.

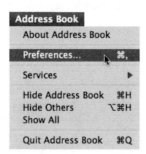

Figure 9.17 From the Address Book menu, choose Preferences to open the Address Book Preferences.

Figure 9.18 The Address Book Preferences window is where you make changes to how the local version of Address Book behaves; it's also where you set up Address Book sharing.

Figure 9.19 You'll use the Sharing preferences pane to control who can access your Address Book information.

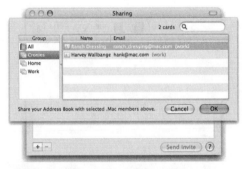

Figure 9.20 When you click the plus (+) button in the Sharing pane, a dialog listing the available Address Book contacts slides down. Select a .Mac member with whom you want to share your Address Book information, and click OK.

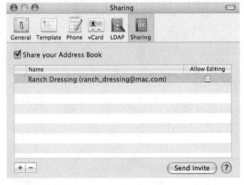

Figure 9.21 Once you've added a .Mac member to the sharing list, that person's name appears in the Sharing pane.

3. At the top of the window, click the Sharing button.

The Sharing pane opens (**Figure 9.19**).

4. Check the "Share your Address Book" box.

Address Book sets up sharing behind the scenes over the course of a few seconds.

5. In the lower left corner of the Sharing pane, click the plus (+) button.

A dialog listing Address Book contacts slides down (**Figure 9.20**).

6. Select the .Mac member or members with whom you want to share your Address Book information, and click OK.

The dialog slides back up, and the selected contact can access your Address Book information (**Figure 9.21**).

continues on next page

7. If you want to allow the .Mac member to edit your Address Book information, check the Allow Editing box to the right of the name (**Figure 9.22**).

8. If you want to send an e-mail invitation to the .Mac member with whom you're sharing your Address Book information, click the Send Invite button in the lower right corner of the Sharing preferences pane.

A new e-mail with an invitation and a link to subscribe to your Address Book is generated in your default e-mail program (**Figure 9.23**). Send it when you're ready.

9. Click the red close button in the upper left corner of the Sharing preferences pane to close the window and save your changes.

✔ Tips

■ Before you can share your Address Book with another .Mac member, that person's contact information (more specifically, his or her *@mac.com* e-mail address) must be entered in your Address Book application.

■ To remove someone from your authorized list of those who can share your Address Book information, click the minus (−) button in the lower left corner of the Sharing preferences pane.

Figure 9.22 Checking the Allow Editing box to the right of a .Mac member's name enables that member to edit your contact information.

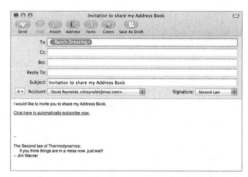

Figure 9.23 When you click Send Invite, an e-mail message is automatically generated in your default e-mail program. This message is addressed to the person who is authorized to share your Address Book information.

Figure 9.24 Choose Subscribe to Address Book from Address Book's File menu to begin the subscription process.

Figure 9.25 Address Book asks for the e-mail address of the .Mac member to whose Address Book information you want to subscribe. Type in the e-mail address and click OK.

Figure 9.26 Once you've subscribed to a .Mac member's Address Book, it appears in the left column of the main Address Book window.

To subscribe to another .Mac member's Address Book:

1. In the Applications folder, double-click the Address Book icon to open the application.

   The main Address Book window opens.

2. From the File menu, choose Subscribe to Address Book (**Figure 9.24**).

   A dialog slides down, asking for the account information of the .Mac member to whose Address Book information you want to subscribe.

3. Type the @*mac.com* e-mail address for the .Mac member in the "Subscribe to this .Mac member's Address Book" field (**Figure 9.25**).

4. Click OK.

   The .Mac member's Address Book appears in the lower left corner of the main Address Book window—in the Group column (**Figure 9.26**). Click the .Mac member's name to open the Address Book.

   continues on next page

SHARING ADDRESS BOOK INFORMATION

✔ Tips

- You can use drag and drop to copy contacts from a shared Address Book into your personal Address Book: In Address Book, click the name of the shared Address Book in the Group column, highlight the name(s) you want to copy, and drag them onto All (or any other name in your personal Group list). If you have edit privileges for a shared Address Book, you can reverse the process to add your contacts to a shared Address Book.

- If you use .Mac Sync with your Address Book contacts, entries in shared Address Books will *not* be copied to your .Mac Address Book, unless you manually copy them to your personal Address Book as described in the previous tip.

- If you receive an e-mail invitation to share another .Mac member's Address Book, click the "Click here to automatically subscribe now" link in the message. Your Address Book application will appear, displaying a prompt confirming the subscription (**Figure 9.27**). Click OK to share that Address Book.

- To unsubscribe from another member's .Mac Address Book information, select the Address Book from which you want to unsubscribe in the main Address Book window, press Delete, and then click Stop when prompted to confirm that you want to cancel the subscription (**Figure 9.28**).

Figure 9.27 If you receive an e-mail invitation to share another .Mac member's Address Book, clicking the embedded "Click here to automatically subscribe now" link will open your Address Book application and display this prompt, asking you to confirm the subscription. Click OK to subscribe.

Figure 9.28 After highlighting the name of a shared Address Book and pressing the Delete key, you must click Stop at this prompt to end your subscription.

Using .Mac
Bookmarks

If you use Safari as your Web browser, you can take advantage of one of .Mac's nifty information-synchronization features: the ability to share a common set of browser bookmarks among several different Macs, and have those bookmarks available online from just about any Web browser.

This synchronization of bookmarks is a real time- and frustration-saver if you have more than one Mac, as anyone who's ever tried to keep bookmarks organized between two or more machines knows.

It's also a real boon for anyone who travels without the benefit of taking along his or her main computer (or any computer). With .Mac bookmark synchronization, your bookmarks are never any farther away than a Web browser and an Internet connection.

The only drawback with .Mac Bookmarks is that you have to use Safari in order to take advantage of them—too bad for the Firefox, Camino, Opera, Microsoft Internet Explorer, Netscape Navigator, Mozilla, and OmniWeb users among us.

In this chapter, I'll show you how to access your Safari bookmarks using a Web browser, add a bookmark, and remove bookmarks and folders. I'll also show you how to set your preferences so that your bookmarks behave the way you want them to.

Accessing Your .Mac Bookmarks

Once you have .Mac synchronization set up properly—as explained in Chapter 8, "Using .Mac Sync"—and you've synchronized your bookmarks, calendars, contacts, keychains, and mail information between your Macintosh and your .Mac account, the bookmarks from Safari on your synchronized computer will be available through your .Mac account, waiting for you to use them.

To access your .Mac Bookmarks:

1. At www.mac.com, log in to your .Mac account (**Figure 10.1**).

   The main .Mac welcome page opens, with you logged in (**Figure 10.2**).

Figure 10.1 Enter your .Mac member name and password in the respective fields, and then click Login to log in to .Mac.

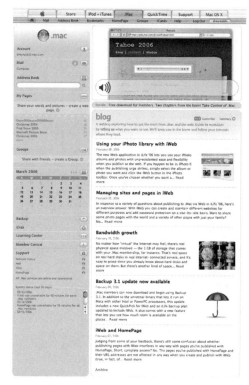

Figure 10.2 This is the main .Mac welcome page, which shows me as being logged in.

Figure 10.3 Click the Bookmarks link at the top of the page.

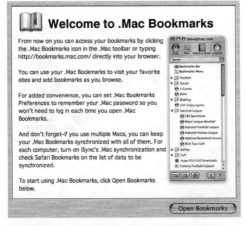

Figure 10.4 The Welcome to .Mac Bookmarks page gives you basic information on how to use .Mac bookmarks, as well as how to synchronize them.

2. At the top of the page, click the Bookmarks link (**Figure 10.3**).

The Welcome to .Mac Bookmarks page opens (**Figure 10.4**). The first time you visit the .Mac Bookmarks page, you may be notified that your bookmarks will be synchronized. This is OK.

continues on next page

3. At the bottom of the page, click the Open Bookmarks button.

Your .Mac Bookmarks window opens, listing the Safari bookmarks synchronized with your computer (**Figure 10.5**). The original browser window reloads the main .Mac members' page.

4. To use these bookmarks, click one of them.

A new browser window opens and loads the Web site of the clicked bookmark (**Figure 10.6**).

Figure 10.5 The .Mac Bookmarks window loads as a separate browser window that can be conveniently pulled to the side of your main browser window.

Figure 10.6 When you click a bookmark in the .Mac Bookmarks window, a new full-size browser window opens and loads the Web site of the clicked bookmark.

Figure 10.7 Click the icon of a collection (one of the items with the folder icon) to open it and load its contents.

Figure 10.8 Bookmark collections can contain folders or bookmarks, or a mix of the two.

5. To open a collection (one of the items indicated by a folder icon), click its icon in the .Mac Bookmarks window (**Figure 10.7**). Don't let the term *collection* throw you—it's really just a top-level folder to help organize your bookmarks.

The collection's contents are loaded in the window (**Figure 10.8**). These can include folders and bookmarks.

continues on next page

ACCESSING YOUR .MAC BOOKMARKS

6. To open a folder, click it.

The disclosure triangle to the left of the folder icon rotates to point down, and the folder's contents are listed in the window (**Figure 10.9**).

7. To view another .Mac Bookmarks collection, choose its name from the pop-up menu below the toolbar (**Figure 10.10**). The selected collection loads.

✔ Tips

■ You can also load your .Mac Bookmarks by going to http://bookmarks.mac.com using a Web browser.

■ You can quickly access other areas of your .Mac account by clicking the .Mac, Mail, and Address Book buttons at the top of your .Mac Bookmarks window.

■ To open the Help page for .Mac Bookmarks, click the question mark button in the lower right corner of the window.

Figure 10.9 When you click the icon for a folder, its contents are listed below, and the disclosure triangle to the left of the folder's name points down.

Figure 10.10 To load a different .Mac Bookmarks collection, choose its name from the pop-up menu at the top of the .Mac Bookmarks window.

Figure 10.11 The Add Bookmark button, at the bottom of the window, is a quick way to add a bookmark to your .Mac Bookmarks.

Figure 10.12 When you click the Add Bookmark button, fields appear where you can add a bookmark name, URL, and location for your new bookmark.

Adding a Bookmark

If you're browsing the Web on someone else's computer, and you run across a site that you really want to bookmark, you can use your .Mac account and whichever Web browser you happen to be using to add that bookmark to your .Mac Bookmarks.

Of course, if you're working on your own computer, it makes more sense to add the bookmark to Safari and it will appear in your .Mac Bookmarks the next time you synchronize your Mac with your .Mac account.

To add a bookmark to your .Mac Bookmarks:

1. Open your .Mac Bookmarks window.

   Your .Mac Bookmarks window opens as shown in Figure 10.5.

2. In the lower left corner of the window, click the Add Bookmark button (**Figure 10.11**). The Add Bookmark button looks like an open book with a plus (+) sign on it.

   The bottom portion of the window expands to show the Add Bookmark fields (**Figure 10.12**).

   continues on next page

ADDING A BOOKMARK

3. In the Add Bookmark fields, *do the following* (**Figure 10.13**):

▲ Click In the Bookmark Name field, type in a short descriptive name for the new bookmark.

▲ In the Bookmark URL field, type in the URL for the Web page you want to bookmark.

▲ From the Add Bookmark To pop-up menu, select the collection to which you want to add the bookmark.

4. Click the Add button.

The .Mac Bookmarks page reloads, complete with the new bookmark; you may have to open a collection to see your new addition, depending on where you saved it (**Figure 10.14**). The next time you synchronize, your new bookmark will be added to Safari in the collection you specified.

✔ Tip

■ When using the .Mac Bookmarks window's Add Bookmark function in Safari (and some other browsers), you can copy the URL of the page in the main browser window by clicking in that window's address field and dragging the highlighted URL to the Bookmark URL field in the .Mac Bookmarks window.

Figure 10.13 After you've filled in the relevant field for your new bookmark, click the Add button to create it.

Figure 10.14 Your newly added bookmark appears in the collection you specified, ready for your use.

Figure 10.15 The Add Folder button, at the bottom of the window, lets you quickly add a folder for new bookmarks.

Adding a Bookmark Folder

Although you can't use the .Mac Web site for full bookmark management—that is, you can't use it to rename, move, or copy bookmarks or folders—you can use it for rudimentary organization by creating folders for bookmarks.

To add a .Mac Bookmarks folder:

1. Open your .Mac Bookmarks window.

2. At the bottom of the window, click the Add Folder button (**Figure 10.15**). It looks like a file folder with a plus (+) sign on it.

   The bottom portion of the window expands to show the Add Folder options (**Figure 10.16**).

continues on next page

Figure 10.16 When you click the Add Folder button, a field and a pop-up menu appear, allowing you to enter a name and choose a location for your new folder.

3. In the Add Folder options, *do the following* (**Figure 10.17**):

▲ In the Folder Name field, type in a short descriptive name for the new folder.

▲ From the Add Folder To pop-up menu, choose the collection (or folder within a collection) to which you want to add the folder.

4. Click Add.

The .Mac Bookmarks window reloads, complete with the new folder; you may have to open a collection or folders within a collection to see your new creation, depending on where you created it (**Figure 10.18**).

✔ Tips

■ To add a bookmark to a newly created bookmark folder, click the Add Bookmark button and choose the new folder from the Add Bookmark To popup menu.

■ You can further organize your .Mac Bookmarks by first making the changes in Safari and then synchronizing your bookmarks with your .Mac account.

Figure 10.17 The Add Folder button, at the bottom of the window, lets you quickly add a folder for new bookmarks.

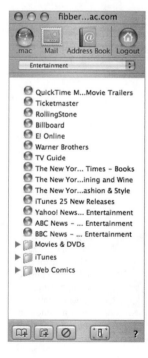

Figure 10.18 Your new folder appears in the appropriate collection, ready for your use.

Figure 10.19 The Delete button at the bottom of the window lets you delete a bookmark or folder.

Figure 10.20 When you click the Delete button, small circles with white embedded Xs appear to the left of all visible items. These are individual Delete buttons.

Removing Bookmarks and Folders

.Mac allows you to remove bookmarks as well as add them—a blessing for those who need to do a little pruning in an overly large collection. You can use this feature to delete either an individual bookmark or a whole folder.

To delete a .Mac Bookmarks folder or bookmark:

1. Open your .Mac Bookmarks window.

2. Navigate to the location that contains the bookmark or folder you want to delete.

3. Click the Delete button at the bottom of the window (**Figure 10.19**). The Delete button looks like a circle with a line through it.

   Delete buttons—circles with embedded white Xs—appear next to each item in the window (**Figure 10.20**).

continues on next page

4. Click the Delete button next to the item you want to delete.

The bottom portion of the window expands to ask if you are sure you want to delete the item (**Figure 10.21**).

5. Click Delete.

The .Mac Bookmarks window reloads with the deleted item removed (**Figure 10.22**). The next time you synchronize your bookmarks with your .Mac account, the deleted item will be removed from your Safari bookmarks.

✔ Tip

■ You can delete only one bookmark or folder at a time, so if you want to do some serious spring cleaning, you may have to repeat this process several times. You might consider making the changes in Safari instead, and then synchronizing your bookmarks.

Figure 10.21 When you click an item's Delete button, a message appears at the bottom of the window asking if you're sure you want to delete the item. Click Delete.

Figure 10.22 After you confirm that you do indeed want to delete the selected item, the .Mac Bookmarks window reloads with the item removed.

REMOVING BOOKMARKS AND FOLDERS

Setting Bookmark Preferences

As with most other aspects of your .Mac account, you can customize how .Mac handles bookmark display and synchronization by setting your .Mac Bookmarks preferences (**Figure 10.23**).

To open the .Mac Bookmarks preferences window, log in to your .Mac account and open the .Mac Bookmarks window; then click the Preferences button in the lower right corner (it's the one that looks like a light switch). This loads the .Mac Bookmarks preferences window, the settings of which you can change as follows:

◆ **Always open pages in a new browser window.** If it's not already selected, click this radio button to cause pages opened from your .Mac Bookmarks to open in a new browser window instead of your current browser window. This is the default setting.

◆ **Always open pages in the same browser window.** Click this radio button to cause pages opened from your .Mac Bookmarks to open in your current browser window.

◆ **Default folder to open.** By default, the All Collections folder is opened when you open your .Mac Bookmarks window (this simply sets your view to the top level of your bookmarks). You can, however, specify a different folder to open by default, by choosing it from the "Default folder to open" pop-up menu.

◆ **Language.** Your .Mac Bookmarks can be displayed in either English or Japanese—you choose which one from the Language pop-up menu.

◆ **Turn on .Mac Bookmarks Synchronization.** This option lets you determine whether your .Mac Bookmarks are synchronized. When you check this box, changes you make to your .Mac Bookmarks are reflected on computers subscribed to this .Mac account.

After you've made your changes to your .Mac Bookmarks preferences, click Save to apply them.

Figure 10.23 The .Mac Bookmarks preferences window lets you customize your .Mac Bookmarks experience by choosing how links open, what collection opens by default, the default language, and whether bookmarks are synchronized.

REMOVING BOOKMARKS AND FOLDERS

USING iCAL

iCal, Apple's free calendaring software, is included with Mac OS X 10.4 Tiger and offers some unique features to .Mac members. Anyone running Mac OS X can use iCal to keep track of calendar events, set alarms for events, and create and manage to-do lists, but .Mac members can also publish their calendars using their .Mac accounts so that anyone with a Web browser can view them. In addition, other Mac OS X users can subscribe to iCal calendars you publish on .Mac, so that the published calendars appear inside their copies of iCal, next to all their other calendars—and can even be automatically updated when changes occur.

In this chapter, I'll show you how to publish your calendars, view your calendars using a Web browser, subscribe to other calendars, and remove calendars.

Publishing Calendars

iCal paired with a .Mac account is a powerful combination. With it, you can publish your calendars on your .Mac account so that others can see your schedule and the events you have planned. As a side benefit, you can also view your calendars from anywhere that you have access to a Web browser.

To publish a calendar:

1. In the Applications folder, double-click the iCal icon to open the application.

   The main iCal window opens (**Figure 11.1**).

2. From the Calendars section on the left, select the calendar you want to publish.

3. From the Calendar menu, choose Publish (**Figure 11.2**).

   A dialog slides down that lets you control what information is published, as well as where it's published.

4. In the dialog, *do the following* (**Figure 11.3**):

   ▲ In the "Publish calendar as" field, type a name for your calendar. Refrain from using non-alphanumeric characters (such as spaces), or you'll have to use the HTML-code equivalents of those characters. For example, a calendar titled My Calendar becomes My%20 Calendar when listed in a URL. This is simply because URLs can't contain spaces, so the space in the calendar name is encoded as *%20*. Bottom line: Avoid non-alphanumeric characters when naming calendars you want to publish.

   ▲ From the "Publish on" pop-up menu, choose .Mac, if it's not already selected.

Figure 11.1 iCal's main interface is pretty simple: familiar visual calendar with all scheduled events on the right, and individual calendars listed on the left. Select a calendar in the list to prepare to publish it.

Figure 11.2 When you choose Publish from the Calendar menu, the calendar-publishing dialog opens; it allows you to name the calendar, specify where it will be published, and indicate what calendar elements will be published.

Figure 11.3 Once you've customized how your calendar will be published, click Publish.

PUBLISHING CALENDARS

Figure 11.4 After you've published a calendar, the Calendar Published dialog appears, giving you several options on what to do next. You can visit the calendar's page, send an e-mail announcing the page, or simply dismiss the dialog by clicking OK.

▲ If you want your published calendar to reflect changes you make to it in iCal, check the "Publish changes automatically" box.

▲ To publish the titles and notes for the calendar's events, check the "Publish titles and notes" box.

▲ To publish alarms associated with the selected calendar, check the "Publish alarms" box.

▲ To publish To Do items associated with the calendar, check the "Publish To Do items" box.

5. Click Publish.

The calendar is uploaded to your .Mac account, and the Calendar Published dialog opens (**Figure 11.4**). This dialog provides the URL for subscribing to the calendar, as well as the URL for viewing the calendar using a Web browser.

continues on next page

PUBLISHING CALENDARS

6. Click the Visit Page button to open the calendar in your Web browser (**Figure 11.5**).

or

Click the Send Mail button to generate an e-mail message announcing the calendar in your default e-mail client (**Figure 11.6**).

or

Click OK to dismiss the dialog.

✔ Tips

■ If you have private calendars that you want to keep secure, don't publish them on your .Mac account where anyone with a Web browser who knows the URLs can view them.

■ You can also publish calendars to private servers with iCal. Choose Calendar > Publish. In the dialog that slides down, choose "a Private Server" from the "Publish on" pop-up menu. This is useful if you want to keep your calendars private, such as with an intranet. Remember—.Mac calendars are neither private nor secure.

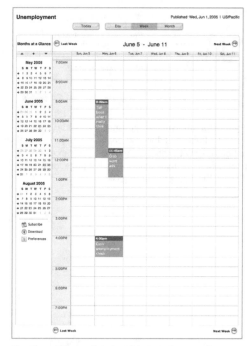

Figure 11.5 If you click the Visit Page button after publishing a calendar, the calendar opens in your Web browser.

Figure 11.6 If you click the Send Mail button after publishing a calendar, an e-mail message is automatically generated in your e-mail client, complete with the details concerning your new calendar.

Figure 11.7 Calendars that you've published show a small icon to the right of their names that looks like a wave emanating from a point.

Figure 11.8 To unpublish a calendar, select the calendar and then choose Unpublish from the Calendar menu.

Figure 11.9 Before you can unpublish a calendar, iCal first asks if you're sure you want to do that. Click Unpublish.

To unpublish a calendar:

1. In the Applications folder, double-click the iCal icon to open the application.

   The main iCal window opens; in the Calendars section on the left, published calendars have a small icon to the right of their names indicating that they have been published (**Figure 11.7**).

2. In the Calendars section, select the calendar you want to unpublish.

3. From the Calendar menu, choose Unpublish (**Figure 11.8**).

   A dialog appears, asking you to confirm that you want to unpublish the calendar (**Figure 11.9**).

4. Click Unpublish.

   The calendar is no longer published on your .Mac account, and the published icon disappears (**Figure 11.10**).

Figure 11.10 After you've unpublished a calendar, the published icon no longer appears to the right of its name in the Calendars column.

Removing an Orphaned Calendar

It's important to note that if you delete an iCal calendar without unpublishing it (say you forget to unpublish it before deleting it), you won't be able to make changes to it. Others, however, will still be able to subscribe to the last published version of that calendar.

To get rid of one of these orphaned calendars, *do the following:*

1. Create a new calendar in iCal with the same name as the published calendar you deleted.

2. Publish the new calendar with the same name as your old calendar. This will replace the existing calendar in your .Mac account.

3. Unpublish the newly created calendar, as described in "To unpublish a calendar."

4. Delete the newly created calendar from iCal.

The orphaned calendar will be replaced with the newly created faux calendar when you publish it (just as an empty file with the same name replaces a large one). Then, when you unpublish it, the faux calendar comes off of .Mac, leaving no trace of itself or its predecessor.

Figure 11.11 To subscribe to an iCal calendar, choose Subscribe from the Calendar menu.

Figure 11.12 To subscribe to an iCal calendar, enter its URL in the "Subscribe to" field. The URL should begin with *webcal://*.

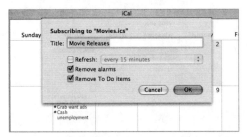

Figure 11.13 In the "Subscribing to" dialog, you can give the calendar a name, set how often it's checked for new information, and set whether alarms and To Do items are also subscribed to.

Subscribing to Calendars

You can use iCal to subscribe to a calendar that someone else (or you, if you like) has published to a .Mac account. This imports the calendar into your copy of iCal, so that you can view that calendar without opening a Web browser. You can customize the update frequency for the subscription and remove alarms and To Do items.

To subscribe to a calendar:

1. In the Applications folder, double-click the iCal icon to open the application.

   The main iCal window opens.

2. From the Calendar menu, choose Subscribe (Command-Option-S) (**Figure 11.11**).

   The "Subscribe to" dialog slides down.

3. In the "Subscribe to" field, type the URL of the calendar you're subscribing to (**Figure 11.12**).

   The URL should begin with *webcal://*.

4. Click Subscribe.

   The calendar is downloaded, and the "Subscribing to" dialog appears, asking you to customize the subscription.

5. In the "Subscribing to" dialog, *do the following* (**Figure 11.13**):

   ▲ In the Title field, type a title for the calendar (one is supplied for you).

   ▲ If you want to have your calendar automatically updated, check the Refresh box.

   continues on next page

▲ From the Refresh pop-up menu, choose a frequency for the updates. Your choices are "every 15 minutes," "every hour," "every day," and "every week."

▲ To remove all alarms from the calendar, check the "Remove alarms" box.

▲ To remove To Do items from the calendar, check the "Remove To Do items" box.

6. Click OK.

The calendar is added to the bottom of iCal's Calendars column on the left side of the window (**Figure 11.14**).

✔ Tips

■ To find out the URL of a calendar, you can do the following: combine *webcal://ical. mac.com/* with the .Mac member name, a slash, the calendar's published name, and finally *.ics*. So, the URL for a .Mac member named bigbill who has published a calendar named Parties would look like webcal://ical.mac.com/bigbill/Parties.ics. Or, you could just ask bigbill, who would be happy to give you his Parties calendar URL.

■ You can find more calendars to subscribe to at www.apple.com/macosx/features/ical/library and www.icalshare.com.

Figure 11.14 Once you've subscribed to a calendar, it appears in the Calendars section of your iCal page.

Figure 11.15 Before you can unsubscribe from a calendar—that is, delete it from your list—iCal asks if you're sure this is something you want to do. Click Delete to proceed.

Figure 11.16 After you've removed a calendar to which you've subscribed, it no longer shows up in the Calendars section.

To unsubscribe from a calendar:

1. In the Applications folder, double-click the iCal icon to open the application.

   The main iCal window opens.

2. From the Calendars section of the window on the left, select the calendar you want to unsubscribe from.

3. Press the Delete key.

   A dialog opens, asking if you're sure you want to remove the calendar (**Figure 11.15**).

4. Click Delete.

   You are unsubscribed from the calendar, and it is removed from your iCal calendar (**Figure 11.16**).

Viewing Calendars Online

When you publish a calendar from iCal on your .Mac account, you can view it using a Web browser. A corollary to this is that you can view any published iCal calendar using a Web browser, provided you know the name of the calendar and the member name of the person who published it.

To view an iCal calendar online:

1. Open your Web browser.

2. In the address field, enter `http://ical. mac.com/`*membername*`/`*calendarname* and press Return—replacing *membername* with the .Mac member name of the person who published the iCal calendar, and *calendarname* with the name of the calendar you want to view.

   The calendar opens in your Web browser, showing the Week view by default (**Figure 11.17**).

3. To view the calendar one day at a time, click the Day button.

   The calendar switches to Day view (**Figure 11.18**).

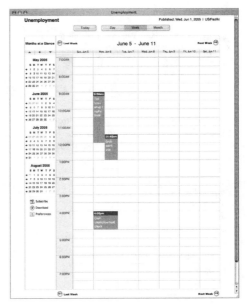

Figure 11.17 When you open a calendar in your Web browser, the Week view is selected by default.

Figure 11.18 Click the Day button to change the calendar to the Day view. A calendar's Day view lets you see how things are supposed to play out each day, minute by minute.

Figure 11.19 A calendar's Month view displays an entire month at a time, with a summary of the month's scheduled events at the bottom.

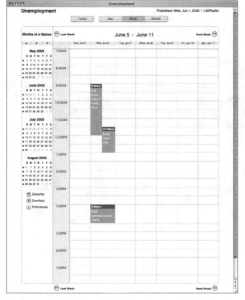

Figure 11.20 The Week view (a calendar's default view) shows the week at a glance, and provides a time frame for each event—a nice cross between the Day and Month views.

4. To view the calendar one month at a time, click the Month button.

The calendar switches to Month view (**Figure 11.19**).

5. To view today's calendar, click the Today button.

The calendar for the day you're working in opens.

6. To view the calendar one week at a time, click the Week button.

The calendar switches to Week view (**Figure 11.20**).

Set Online Calendar Preferences

You can set a calendar's viewing preferences by clicking the Preferences button in the lower left column of the calendar's Web page (**Figure 11.21**). When this page opens (**Figure 11.22**), you can alter the following settings:

◆ **Choose a language.** From the "Choose a language" pop-up menu, choose which of 15 languages the calendar is displayed in.

◆ **Choose whether the event list is displayed.** From the "Event list" pop-up menu, choose On or Off to set whether the event list appears at the bottom of the calendar in Month view.

◆ **Choose a default calendar view.** From the "Default calendar" pop-up menu, select Daily, Weekly, or Monthly to set which view is the default.

◆ **Choose the day on which the week starts.** From the "Start week on" pop-up menu, choose a day of the week on which you want calendars to start. By default, this is set to Sunday, but no one's stopping you from setting it to Thursday if you like.

◆ **Choose how the time is displayed.** From the "Time display" pop-up menu, choose whether calendars are displayed using a 12-hour or 24-hour clock.

Once you've made your selections, click the Apply button in the lower right corner to save your changes.

Figure 11.21 Click the Preferences button to load the preferences for that Web calendar.

Figure 11.22 On the calendar preferences page, you can change some settings that govern how the calendar behaves—such as the language it's displayed in, whether the event list is shown, and what the default calendar view looks like.

VIEWING CALENDARS ONLINE

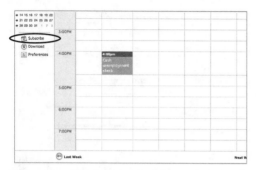

Figure 11.23 Click the Subscribe button to launch iCal and subscribe to the calendar you're viewing in your Web browser.

Figure 11.24 After you click Subscribe, the "Subscribe to" dialog slides down, with the URL for the calendar you were just viewing filled in. To subscribe, click the Subscribe button.

Figure 11.25 To download a file of the calendar (in a format that can be read by some other calendaring programs, such as Microsoft Entourage), click the Download button.

To subscribe to a calendar online:

1. Open your Web browser.

2. In the address field, enter `http://ical.mac.com/`*membername*`/`*calendarname*, and press Return—replacing *membername* with the .Mac member name of the person publishing the iCal calendar, and replacing *calendarname* with the name of the calendar you want to view.

   The calendar opens in your Web browser.

3. In the left column, click the Subscribe button (**Figure 11.23**).

   iCal opens and presents you with the "Subscribe to" dialog, with the URL filled in automatically (**Figure 11.24**).

4. Click Subscribe.

   The subscribed calendar appears in iCal.

To download a calendar:

1. Open a calendar in a Web browser.

2. In the lower left column, click the Download button (**Figure 11.25**).

   A calendar file downloads to the folder where files are normally downloaded. You can import this calendar file into calendaring programs that don't support subscriptions, such as Microsoft Entourage.

continues on next page

✔ Tips

- To import a calendar file into another program, typically you can either drop the calendar file on the program's icon, or import the file through the program's import function.

- To view more information about a calendar event, click it in the browser window. A window pops up with details about the event (**Figure 11.26**).

- You can browse through a calendar by clicking the Last and Next buttons at the top and bottom of the calendar's browser window (**Figure 11.27**).

- To view an individual day, click it in the Months at a Glance sidebar. The day will load in the browser window.

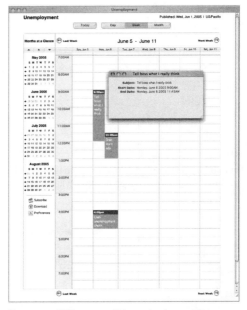

Figure 11.26 When you click a calendar event, a window pops up with more information about that event, showing its title, start date, and end date.

Figure 11.27 To browse through a calendar, click the Last and Next buttons at the top and bottom of the calendar's browser window.

12

Using Backup

One of the many perks of having a .Mac account is that you get a copy of Apple's file-backup program—named, appropriately, Backup. With it, you can set up your system to automatically copy important files to your iDisk, to a network volume or another hard drive, or even burn them to CD or DVD.

The information on your computer—all of your e-mail messages, letters, digital photos, everything—is there because incredibly complex electronic devices and equally complex software keep everything in order. But, inevitably, something happens to one of those systems, and precious data evaporates. It happened to me personally. Twice.

Backup offers hope. Properly used, it's a great way to ensure that you don't lose any valuable data. Once you've set up a backup scheme, Backup copies the latest versions of all your files, so that if something happens to your "working" copy, you can easily restore it from the backup copy. In this chapter, I'll show you how to set up Backup to protect your data.

And for those of you using Backup 3, a little note—although there's a lot of Backup 2 instructions here, don't lose heart. Although Backup 3 is more powerful to use, it's also easier to use, and so it requires less in the way of step-by-step instructions.

Installing Backup

Backup comes in two flavors: version 3 (or 3.1 at this writing), for Mac OS X 10.3.9 and 10.4.2 or later; and version 2 (technically 2.0.2), for Mac OS X 10.2.6. If your Mac starts up using an older version of Mac OS X or Mac OS 9, you are out of luck on this one; but if you run Mac OS 9 software in Classic mode under Mac OS X 10.2 or later, you can use Backup to safeguard the files those programs create.

To use Backup, you need a .Mac account member name and password—from a paid .Mac subscription, a trial account, or an expired account (including an expired trial account). As you might expect, Backup's features are somewhat limited for non-paid accounts: When Backup 3 is used with such an account, it cannot back up a file or folder that exceeds 100 MB in size (while there's no size limit for paid subscriptions). When Backup 2 is used with a trial subscription or expired account, the only location where it can place backed-up files is your iDisk; backing up to hard disks and recordable CDs or DVDs requires a paid subscription. Be sure your .Mac member name and password are entered in the .Mac section of System Preferences.

Backup's user interface is pretty basic—it asks where you want your backup files stored and shows you how much space is available there. It also lets you select what groups of files to back up, as well as add items, refresh your list, schedule backups, and eject the volume to which you're backing up all your files.

But first you must download and install the Backup software.

Backup Strategy

A good backup strategy involves making two or more backups, preferably stored in two or more locations. That way, if your main computer and one of your backups is destroyed, you'll have a second copy. Sure, it sounds redundant, but here's an example: You've made a backup of your computer to DVD, and you've stored it in your basement. Then you have a house fire that starts in your basement and consumes not only your backup, but your computer, too. Do yourself a favor—make two or more backups and put them in different physical locations, especially for important things such as financial data.

Figure 12.1 Before you can download the Backup software, you'll need to log in to your .Mac account by entering your .Mac member name and password.

Figure 12.2 Click the Backup link from the main page to go to the Backup download and information page.

To download and install Backup 3:

1. Using a Web browser, log in to your .Mac account (**Figure 12.1**).

   The main .Mac Web page loads.

2. On the left side of the page, click Backup (**Figure 12.2**).

   The Backup 3 page loads.

continues on next page

3. In the main banner of the page (toward the left), click "Download Backup 3 now" (**Figure 12.3**).

The main Backup download page loads. Here, you're presented with a choice of which version of Backup to download—2.0.2 or 3.1.

4. If you're using Mac OS X 10.2.6, click the link to download Backup 2.0.2. If you're using either Mac OS X 10.3.9 or version 10.4.2 or later, click the link to download Backup 3 (**Figure 12.4**).

Backup is downloaded to your hard drive in the location to which you normally download files.

5. Once the disk-image file downloads to your hard drive, mount it by double-clicking it (if it's not automatically mounted).

The disk image mounts (**Figure 12.5**).

Figure 12.3 The Backup page contains links to download the Backup software, as well as links to pages that provide in-depth information on the program.

Figure 12.4 The Backup download page has download links for two versions of Backup: Backup 2 and Backup 3. Click the download link for the version appropriate to your operating system.

Figure 12.5 The Backup disk image contains the installer package for Backup. Double-click its icon to launch the installer.

Figure 12.6 The Backup installer's Welcome pane gives you an overview of Backup. Click Continue to move on to the next step.

Figure 12.7 The Important Information pane contains valuable information about how to install and use Backup. Read it and click Continue.

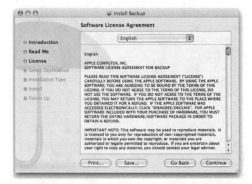

Figure 12.8 The Backup Software License Agreement is a legal document—it's worth reading this to see what you're agreeing to. Click Continue to move on.

6. Open the Backup disk image, and then double-click the Backup.pkg icon to launch the Backup installer.

   The Welcome pane appears (**Figure 12.6**).

7. Click Continue.

   The Important Information pane opens; it contains valuable information about installing and using Backup (**Figure 12.7**).

8. Click Continue.

   The Backup Software License Agreement pane opens (**Figure 12.8**).

continues on next page

9. Click Continue.

A dialog slides down, noting that in order to continue to install Backup, you must agree to the terms of the license agreement (**Figure 12.9**).

10. Click Agree.

The Select a Destination pane opens; it lists all available locations where you can install Backup (**Figure 12.10**).

11. Select a destination volume and click Continue.

The Installation Type pane loads (**Figure 12.11**).

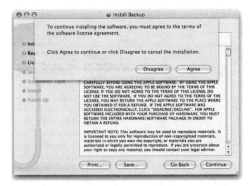

Figure 12.9 To continue with the installation, you must click the Agree button in the Software License Agreement pane.

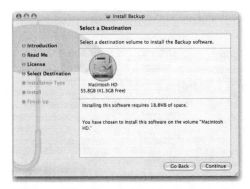

Figure 12.10 The Select a Destination pane lists all valid locations for a Backup installation. Select the one you want (usually your main hard drive) and click Continue.

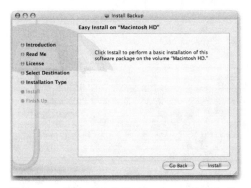

Figure 12.11 In the Installation Type pane, there isn't much to do, since Backup doesn't have any installation options. Click Install.

Figure 12.12 Before you can install Backup, you must type in your administrator password and click OK.

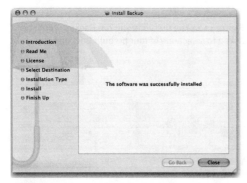

Figure 12.13 Click the Close button to complete the installation of Backup.

12. Click Install.

The Authenticate dialog opens (**Figure 12.12**).

13. Type your system password and click OK.

The installer installs Backup in the Applications folder of your hard drive and does some other housekeeping. When it's finished, a message appears, noting that Backup has finished installing.

14. Click Close (**Figure 12.13**).

Backup is now installed in your Applications folder.

✔ Tip

■ Backup is fussier than most applications about requiring the latest, greatest update of whichever version of Mac OS X it runs under. If you're using Backup 2 with Mac OS X 10.2 Jaguar, you must update to version 10.2.6, and if you're using Backup 3 with Mac OS X 10.3 Panther, you must upgrade to 10.3.9. At this writing, the latest version of Backup 3 (3.1) supports versions of Mac OS X 10.4 Tiger from 10.4.2 on, but for best results with Backup in the future, keep it and your system software up to date, using the Software Update utility found in the Apple menu.

INSTALLING BACKUP

Setting Up Backup 3

Backup 3 makes it easy to set up and run multiple backups to your iDisk, to optical media, or to another hard drive.

When you first open Backup 3, it presents you with a window that lists four Backup plans (**Figure 12.14**):

◆ **Home Folder**—Schedules daily backup of your home folder to your hard drive, as well as monthly backup to CD or DVD

◆ **Personal Data & Settings**—Backs up basic personal information (such as Address Book contacts and Safari settings) every day

◆ **iLife**—Backs up your iLife data every week to CD or DVD

◆ **Purchased Music and Video**—Backs up music and video that you've purchased using iTunes to a CD or DVD every month

While you don't *have* to choose one of these Backup plans, it's probably a good idea to go with one—or with all of them.

Check the box next to the plan you want to choose. A great place to start is with the Home Folder plan (**Figure 12.15**). Click Continue.

The main Backup window opens, listing details for the plan you just created, as well as information about when the plan has run and when it's scheduled to run again.

✔ Tips

■ A Backup plan is simply a description of what files and folders get backed up, where they get backed up, and how often they get backed up.

Figure 12.14 The first time you run Backup, you'll be asked to select one of four prebuilt Backup plans.

Figure 12.15 The Home Folder plan backs up the files in your home folder, covering most of your backup needs in one swoop.

■ Backup plans apply only to data that the user who sets up the plan has access to—mostly that user's home folder, but any readable file is fair game. If more than one person has a user account on your Mac, each will have to set up backups to protect his or her files, and each will need his or her own .Mac account to do so.

Figure 12.16 The main Backup window lists any existing backup plans you've created. Since this is the first time Backup has run, it shows only one plan: Home Folder.

Figure 12.17 Click the plus button to open the plan template window.

Figure 12.18 The plan template window gives you the option of choosing one of four premade templates.

To create a backup from a plan template:

Backup includes several preconfigured templates that fill many backup needs. Here's how to create a backup using one of these templates:

1. Open the Backup application.

   The main Backup window is displayed, showing any plans that have already been set up (**Figure 12.16**).

2. Click the plus (+) button in the lower left corner (**Figure 12.17**).

   The plan template window is displayed (**Figure 12.18**).

continues on next page

3. In the window, *select one of the following* and then click the Choose Plan button:

▲ Home Folder—If you want to back up the contents of your home folder (a great first choice)

▲ Personal Data & Settings—If you want to back up your Address Book information, iCal information, Safari settings, Stickies, or Mac OS keychains

▲ iLife—If you want to back up your iLife data from your home folder (including GarageBand projects, iDVD projects, iMovie projects, iPhoto library, iTunes library, and iWeb Web sites)

▲ Purchased Music and Video—If you want to back up the music and video you've purchased from the iTunes Music Store

▲ Custom—If you want to select a set of files and use a schedule that you set up from scratch

The detail window for the plan you chose is displayed (**Figure 12.19**).

4. If you choose Custom in the Plan Template Window (see Figure 12.18) you'll be prompted to type a name for the backup plan you're creating.

The name appears at the top of the detail window (**Figure 12.20**).

Figure 12.19 The plan's detail window is displayed, showing the specifics of how the backup plan will proceed.

Figure 12.20 If you create a Custom backup plan, you'll be prompted to type its name in the name field of the plan's detail window.

Figure 12.21 Click the plus button in the lower left corner of the window to open the Choose Items to Back Up window.

Figure 12.22 The Choose Items to Back Up window contains groups of files that you can choose to have backed up.

5. To add an item to be backed up, click the plus (+) button below the Backup Items portion of the window (**Figure 12.21**). The Choose Items to Back Up window appears (**Figure 12.22**).

continues on next page

What Gets Backed Up, Exactly?

If you want to know the details of what's actually backed up with a particular Backup option (either a QuickPick or another folder)—or if you want to fine-tune which files a Backup plan protects—just double-click the item in the Backup Items list. A sidebar drawer opens, revealing more information about what files will be backed up and allowing you to control which files in a group are copied.

To choose whether a file or folder in the selected item will be backed up, highlight it and make sure the "Include this file" or "Include this folder" radio button is selected at the bottom of the drawer window.

From the Show pop-up menu at the bottom of the sidebar, you can select whether General Information (such as the kind, size, and last-modified date) or Backup Information (such as time of last backup) appears below the file list.

In the case of QuickPicks (such as with application files—Microsoft Word or PowerPoint files, and the like), you can check boxes to the left of the individual items to indicate whether those items should be backed up, giving you a great degree of control over QuickPicks and backups of your own file groups.

SETTING UP BACKUP 3

6. While the Choose Items to Back Up window is open, *do any or all of the following:*
To add QuickPicks (a backup of files by type), *do the following:*

▲ Click the QuickPicks tab to load the QuickPicks pane (if it's not already selected).

▲ Check the boxes to the left of the items that you want backed up (if they're not included in the plan) (**Figure 12.23**).

To add individual files and/or folders:

▲ Click the Files & Folders tab to load the Files & Folders pane.

▲ Navigate to a file or folder you want to include in the backup (if it's not included in the original plan).

▲ Click the "Include this folder" radio button (**Figure 12.24**).

To add items via a Spotlight search:

▲ Click the Spotlight tab to open the Spotlight search pane.

▲ Type in the search term you want to use for your Spotlight search.

▲ Click Servers, Computer, or Home to restrict your search to the area that contains the files you want to back up.

▲ Select the files you want to back up.

▲ Click the "Include these items" radio button (**Figure 12.25**).

▲ Click Done.

▲ The selected items will be included in the next backup.

Figure 12.23 Check the boxes to the left of the items you want added to the Backup plan.

Figure 12.24 Change the settings in the Files & Folders pane to create a custom set of files to back up.

Figure 12.25 Use a Spotlight search to find files that you want backed up on a regular basis.

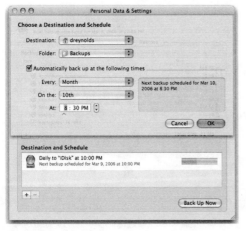

Figure 12.26 The Destination and Schedule pane allows you to choose where files are backed up and when the backup occurs.

7. To change the backup frequency and/or backup-file destination for a preset backup plan, double-click the contentsof the Destination and Schedule field in the detail window for the plan you're tweaking. (If you've created a custom plan, click the plus (+) button beneath the Destination and Schedule field.)

   The Choose a Destination and Schedule pane opens (**Figure 12.26**).

8. *Do the following:*

   ▲ To choose the location where your backup file will be stored, select a disk, the Home folder, a network volume, or iDisk from the Destination pop-up menu.

   ▲ If you don't want the backup located in a folder called Backups in the destination you selected, select Choose Location in the Folder pop-up menu to navigate to a preferred folder and click OK. (This option will not be enabled if you have selected iDisk or CD or DVD).

   ▲ Check the "Automatically back up at the following times" box to have the backup happen at the time indicated below the box.

   ▲ From the Every menu, select whether the backup happens every day, week, month, three months, or six months.

continues on next page

SETTING UP BACKUP 3

▲ If you've selected Week, select the day of the week from the "On the" pop-up menu.

▲ If you've selected Month, select the day of the month from the "On the" popup menu.

▲ In the At section, select the time when you want the backup to occur.

▲ Click OK.

The new schedule appears in the Destination and Schedule area of the window (**Figure 12.27**).

9. Close the window.

Your backup now appears in the list of scheduled backups (**Figure 12.28**).

✔ Tips

■ Backup 3 safeguards your projects and files, but it may not protect the programs used to create them. For example, the iLife backup plan backs up your iPhoto image library (among other things), but not the iPhoto application itself, unless you create a plan that includes the application. The problem with this is that while most applications don't mind being moved or copied, some do, and they may not work properly if restored. So if you ever need to restore an application, use its original installation disc.

■ To set up a schedule and set a destination for the backup other than the preset ones, click the plus button below the Destination and Schedule label and edit the schedule.

■ To delete a schedule, select it and press the Delete key.

■ To perform a backup immediately, select the backup you want to execute, and then click the Back Up button at the bottom of the window.

Figure 12.27 Change the settings in the window to customize where the backup is stored and when it happens.

Figure 12.28 Once you create a Backup plan, it appears in the main Backup window.

Figure 12.29 The main Backup window displays any Backup plans you create.

Figure 12.30 The plan template page allows you to customize your backups as you like.

To edit a Backup plan:

1. Open the Backup application.

   The main Backup window is displayed, showing any plans that have already been set up (**Figure 12.29**).

2. Double-click the Backup plan you want to edit.

   The plan template page is displayed (**Figure 12.30**).

3. Following steps 2–11 of "To create a backup from a plan template," make the changes that you want to the plan.

   After you close the window, the edited plan will be executed on the schedule you set.

To restore a backup:

1. Open the Backup application.

The main Backup window is displayed, showing any plans that have already been set up (see Figure 12.29).

2. Select the backup you want to restore, and click the Restore button (**Figure 12.31**).

The Restore window opens (**Figure 12.32**).

Figure 12.31 To restore files from a backup, select the plan you want to restore from, and click Restore.

Figure 12.32 The Restore window displays the back-ups that have been made from the selected plan.

Figure 12.33 Items within a given backup are listed to the right of the selected backup.

3. In the Previous Backups portion of the window (on the left), select the backup that you want to restore.

The items within that backup are listed to the right of the backup name (**Figure 12.33**).

4. Check the boxes next to the items you want to restore, and click Restore Selection (**Figure 12.34**).

A dialog slides down, asking how you would like to handle the restoration (**Figure 12.35**).

continues on next page

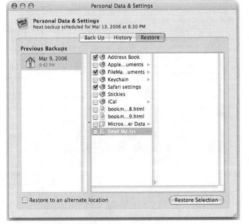

Figure 12.34 Check the boxes of the files you want restored, and click the Restore Selection button.

Figure 12.35 When restoring files from a backup, you will be asked how you want to proceed—either by restoring only missing items or by replacing existing items with backup copies.

SETTING UP BACKUP 3

5. In the dialog, select *one of the following radio buttons:*

▲ "Restore missing items" to restore only items that are no longer in their original locations

▲ "Replace existing items" to restore all items, whether or not they exist in the original location

Click Restore.

If you have any applications running, Backup will warn you to quit those applications before restoring the files, and the items will be restored to your Mac (**Figure 12.36**).

6. Click Continue.

Backup goes to work restoring the files (**Figure 12.37**).

✔ Tips

■ To view the history of a particular backup, select the plan in the main window and then select History from the Plan window. The complete history of that backup is displayed.

■ After the first backup, Backup creates incremental backups—that is, only files that have been changed get backed up. If you want to force a full backup, select the plan in the main Backup window, and then choose Full Backup from the Plan window.

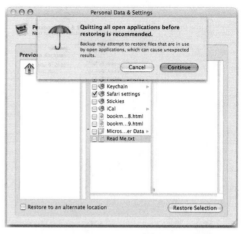

Figure 12.36 To ensure a clean backup, you will need to quit running applications before completing the restoration.

Figure 12.37 After you click Continue, Backup restores the files.

Setting Up Backup 2

The general process of setting up Backup 2 to protect your important data is fairly easy, although there are a number of choices to be made during the process—mostly revolving around where you want your backups to be made.

You have three choices:

- **Back up to iDisk.** This creates a backup on your iDisk over your Internet connection. Choose this option if you have a high-speed Internet connection, and be sure to limit the number of files you back up, or you'll overwhelm your iDisk.

- **Back up to CD/DVD.** This creates a backup on recordable CDs or DVDs using your Mac's CD or DVD burner. Choose this option to create durable backups of your data, but remember—you'll have to be by your Mac during the backup to provide it with blank discs.

- **Back up to Drive.** This creates a backup on another hard drive or network volume. Choose this option to back up your important data to another hard drive or network volume.

When you fire up Backup for the first time, you'll be presented with its default setup. Although Backup can be set up to back up just about any files to just about any location on a schedule, it's not set up that way when you launch it. It's your job to customize these settings to suit your needs. Doing so is a three-step process: choosing where you want the files to be backed up, selecting which files are to be backed up, and setting up a schedule of when backups occur.

Deleting Items from the iDisk Backup

If you've backed up files to your iDisk and you'd like to delete them, no problem. Simply open Backup, and in the pop-up menu in the upper left corner of the window choose Restore from iDisk. Next, check the boxes next to the items you want to delete from the online backup. Press Delete, confirm that you actually want to delete the backup, and the files are gone.

If you want to nuke the whole lot, you can erase all of the items in your .Mac backup by opening the Backup application and, in Backup 3, selecting Remove iDisk Backups from the Backup menu. If you're using Backup 2, choose Clear iDisk Backup Folder from the Edit menu.

In either case, you'll be asked if you really want to go through with it. Click Yes to do the job.

To back up to iDisk with Backup 2:

1. In the Applications folder, double-click the Backup icon to launch the software.

Backup checks for an iDisk server as it launches. If this is the first time you've launched Backup, you may receive a message saying that BackupHelper wants permission to access your keychain (**Figure 12.38**). This is OK. If you've already launched Backup, go to step 3.

2. Click Always Allow.

If this is the first time you've launched Backup, a dialog appears, thanking you for joining .Mac (**Figure 12.39**).

3. Click OK.

Backup displays its main window (**Figure 12.40**).

Figure 12.38 If this is the first time you've launched Backup 2, you may be asked for access to your keychain. This is OK; click Always Allow.

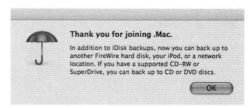

Figure 12.39 If this is the first time you've launched Backup 2, a dialog opens, thanking you for joining .Mac.

Figure 12.40 The main Backup window is a pretty simple affair. It asks where files should be backed up; it provides a graphical representation of how much space is available on your iDisk; it lists the items to be backed up; it provides some information on scheduling and file size; and it has some basic controls, including a Backup Now button.

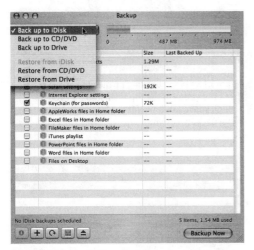

Figure 12.41 The Backup window pop-up menu offers three backup choices: Back up to iDisk, Back up to CD/DVD, and Back up to Drive. You need to choose one of them to create a backup.

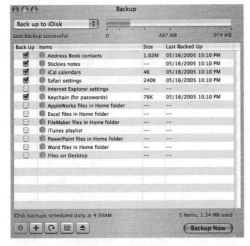

Figure 12.42 When you check the boxes to the left of the items you want to have backed up, Backup will scan your hard drive for those items and automatically include them.

4. From the pop-up menu in the upper left corner, choose Back up to iDisk (**Figure 12.41**).

5. In the Back Up column of the main window, check the boxes to the left of the items that you want to back up (**Figure 12.42**).

continues on next page

SETTING UP BACKUP 2

6. At the top of the window, check the available-space gauge to ensure that you have enough space in which to copy the selected items. This gauge appears when you select Back up to iDisk in step 4 (**Figure 12.43**).

7. In the lower right corner of the window, click the Backup Now button (**Figure 12.44**).

Backup scans for the files to be saved and goes straight to work creating your backup in the location you've specified. You'll see a progress bar as items are copied to the location you set in step 4.

✔ Tip

■ When backing up files to your iDisk, you'll need to have your .Mac member name and password entered in the .Mac pane of System Preferences, and you'll have to have Internet access (which makes sense when you think about it). A backup can potentially take up gigabytes of space, so when backing up to your iDisk, remember that you'll need to make the backup small enough to fit on your iDisk.

Figure 12.43 When backing up files to your iDisk, check the gauge at the top to ensure that you have enough space available for the files you've selected in the Back Up column.

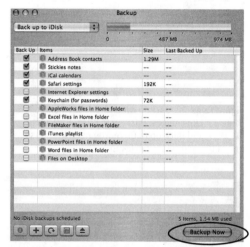

Figure 12.44 Click the Backup Now button to begin your backup.

Figure 12.45 Choose Back up to CD/DVD from the Backup pop-up menu to back up items to optical discs.

Figure 12.46 When you check the boxes to the left of the items you want to have backed up, Backup will scan your hard drive for those items and automatically include them.

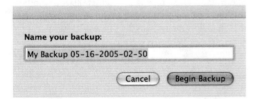

Figure 12.47 Before you back up to CD/DVD media, Backup requires that you give a name to your backup. It provides a good one, though—the current date and time. If you like this name, or after you've typed in a name of your own, click Begin Backup.

Figure 12.48 To continue the backup process, insert a CD and click Burn in the dialog when the button becomes activated.

To back up to a CD or DVD with Backup 2:

1. Open Backup.

   If this is the first time you've launched Backup, you may receive a message saying that BackupHelper wants permission to access your keychain (see Figure 12.38). This is OK. If you've already launched Backup, go to step 3.

2. Click Always Allow.

   If this is the first time you've launched Backup, a dialog appears, thanking you for joining .Mac (see Figure 12.39).

3. Click OK.

   Backup displays its main window.

4. From the pop-up menu in the upper left corner, choose Back up to CD/DVD (**Figure 12.45**).

5. In the Back Up column of the main window, check the boxes to the left of the items that you want to back up (**Figure 12.46**).

6. In the lower right corner of the window, click the Backup Now button.

   A dialog pops up, asking you to name your backup.

7. In the "Name your backup" field, type a name for your backup, and then click Begin Backup (**Figure 12.47**).

   Backup asks you to insert a disc (**Figure 12.48**).

continues on next page

8. Insert a disc.

The Burn button is activated.

9. Click Burn (**Figure 12.49**).

Backup burns the files to the disc that you inserted (**Figure 12.50**). Depending on the size of the backup, you may need to insert more than one disc when asked. When finished with the process, Backup provides a short summary dialog, giving you the name that you should use to label the CD or DVD, and noting how many discs the backup used (**Figure 12.51**).

10. Click OK to finish.

✔ Tips

■ When you back up your data to CDs or DVDs, Backup tells you in advance how many blank disks you'll need.

■ Backup allows backing up to CDs and DVDs only if your Mac has a Mac OS X–supported optical drive—there's a complete list at Mac OS X Storage Device Support (www.apple.com/macosx/upgrade/storage.html).

Figure 12.49 Click the Burn button to burn the backup to CD or DVD.

Figure 12.50 After you click the Burn button, Backup goes to work gathering files and burning them to CD or DVD.

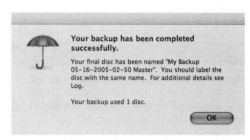

Figure 12.51 When finished, Backup tells you whether the backup process was successful, what to label the disc, and how many discs the process used.

SETTING UP BACKUP 2

Figure 12.52 Select Back up to Drive from the pop-up menu in the Backup window to back up items to hard drives or network volumes.

Figure 12.53 Click the Set button to choose a location on a drive for your backup.

To back up to a drive:

1. Open Backup.

   If this is the first time you've launched Backup, you may receive a message saying that BackupHelper wants permission to access your keychain (see Figure 12.38). This is OK. If you've already launched Backup, go to step 3.

2. Click Always Allow.

   If this is the first time you've launched Backup, a dialog appears, thanking you for joining .Mac (see Figure 12.39).

3. Click OK.

   Backup displays its main window.

4. From the pop-up menu in the upper left corner, choose Back up to Drive (**Figure 12.52**).

5. At the top of the window, click the Set button (**Figure 12.53**).

continues on next page

6. In the "Set a backup location" dialog that drops down, click Create (**Figure 12.54**).

7. In the file browser window that rolls down, navigate to the location you want to use for the backup, type a name for your backup in the Save As field, and click Create (**Figure 12.55**).

Backup displays its main window with the new backup name reflected in the top portion of the window, just to the right of the Set button (**Figure 12.56**).

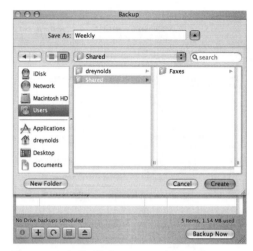

Figure 12.55 In the file browser, navigate to the location you want to use for your backup, give it a name in the Save As field, and click Create. We're calling this backup "Weekly" to indicate how often we'll use it for a backup, but you can name it anything (as long as you use standard alphanumeric characters).

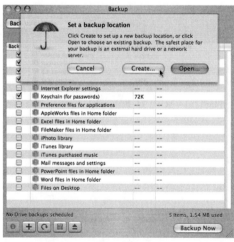

Figure 12.54 Click Create to create a new backup file and set a location in which backups will take place.

Figure 12.56 The main Backup window has your new backup listed at the top. Here, it's named Weekly, but it could be named anything—even "Spike MacRashton."

Figure 12.57 When you check the boxes to the left of the items you want to have backed up, Backup will scan your hard drive for those items and automatically include them.

Figure 12.58 Click the Backup Now button to begin your backup.

8. In the Back Up column, check the boxes of the items that you want to back up (**Figure 12.57**).

9. In the lower right corner of the window, click the Backup Now button (**Figure 12.58**).

   Backup scans for the files to be saved and goes straight to work creating your backup in the location you've specified. You'll see a progress bar as items are copied to the location you set in step 4.

✔ Tip

- Although you can back up your files to the same hard drive, it's not a very good idea. What happens if your drive crashes? You lose your originals and your backup, that's what.

Using Backup 2's QuickPicks

Backup 2 comes prepopulated with a series of items called QuickPicks that make it easy to automate backups. These QuickPicks back up information that's likely to be important—especially information that you may not know the location of (think back to the last time you knew where your Adobe Photoshop preferences or Actions Palette files were stored).

The selection of QuickPicks varies, depending on the backup location you've selected (after all, no one can copy respectable iPhoto and iTunes libraries to an iDisk, the combination of which would be many gigabytes more than an iDisk can hold).

To take advantage of these QuickPicks, simply check the boxes next to the ones you want to use. Backup will do any necessary configuration for you (such as scanning for the files to be included), and the items will be included in the backup.

These QuickPicks cover the following (**Figure 12.59**):

◆ **Address Book contacts.** Backs up the contact information you have stored in Address Book.

◆ **Stickies notes.** If you use Stickies, this QuickPick will back up your notes.

◆ **iCal calendars.** Creates a copy of your iCal calendar information.

◆ **Safari settings.** Backs up your Safari settings and bookmarks, as well as any cache files (this can make your Safari backup larger than it might otherwise be).

◆ **Internet Explorer settings.** Backs up your Microsoft Internet Explorer bookmarks and settings.

Figure 12.59 The Backup interface has a set of file groups, called QuickPicks, that you can use to quickly create a backup.

- **Keychain (for passwords).** Makes a copy of passwords that you've entered in the Keychain application.

- **Preferences** (not available for iDisk backups). Backs up the preference files for all of your applications. This one's a huge deal— it catches all of those files that keep your Mac's applications acting the way you expect.

- **AppleWorks files in Home folder.** Scans all files in your home directory and makes a backup of all AppleWorks files.

- **Excel files in Home folder.** Scans all files in your home directory and makes a backup of all Microsoft Excel files.

- **FileMaker files in Home folder.** Scans all files in your home directory and makes a backup of all FileMaker databases.

- **iPhoto library.** Copies your iPhoto digital photography. Since these backups can be really large, this option isn't available for iDisk backups.

- **iTunes library.** Copies your iTunes music library. Again, since these can be really large backups, this option isn't available for iDisk backups.

- **iTunes playlist.** Makes a copy of any iTunes playlists. This option is only available for iDisk backups.

- **iTunes purchases.** Makes a copy of any iTunes purchased music. This option is not available for iDisk backups.

- **PowerPoint files in Home folder.** Scans all files in your home directory and makes a backup of all PowerPoint files.

- **Word files in Home folder.** Scans all files in your home directory and makes a backup of all Word files.

- **Files on Desktop.** Makes a copy of all the files you keep on your Desktop.

Adding File Groups with Backup 2

Although you can perform a perfectly good backup using just QuickPicks, you can also choose your own collections of files and folders to back up.

To add a file group in Backup 2:

1. Open Backup.

Backup displays its main window.

2. *Do one of the following:*

▲ In the Finder, select the files you want to back up, and drag them into the Backup window (**Figure 12.60**).

▲ In the lower left corner of the main Backup window, click the plus (+) button (**Figure 12.61**) to bring up a file-browser window. Navigate to the folder that you want to back up, and click Choose (**Figure 12.62**).

Figure 12.60 Drag the files or folders (or any combination of them) into the Backup window to add them as QuickPicks.

Figure 12.61 Click the plus (+) button to open a file browser that allows you to choose files or folders to include in a backup group.

Figure 12.62 Once you've navigated to the file or folder you want to include in a file group, click Choose.

Figure 12.63 The file or folder you choose appears at the bottom of the window with its box checked, ready to be included during the next backup.

The items you dragged into the window appear as files and folders below the QuickPicks in the list. These files and folders have checked boxes next to them, indicating that they will be backed up during the next backup operation (**Figure 12.63**).

✔ Tip

■ You can drag files and folders from any Finder window, including a search-results window. To create a backup list of files you search for, perform a search and then drag the items you want to back up from the search-results window into the Backup window.

To remove a file group in Backup 2:

1. Open Backup.

Backup displays its main window.

2. Control-click the file or folder you want to remove.

A contextual menu appears under the pointer with one choice—Delete.

3. Choose Delete from the menu (**Figure 12.64**).

The item is deleted from the list of files to be backed up.

✔ Tips

■ You can also delete an item by selecting it in the window and pressing Delete.

■ If you've got a two-button mouse, you can remove an item from the list of Quick-Picks and folders by right-clicking it. If you delete a standard QuickPick and later decide you want that QuickPick back, choose Edit > Restore All QuickPicks.

Figure 12.64 Choosing Delete from the contextual menu brought up by Control-clicking an item deletes the item from the QuickPick list.

Figure 12.65 Click the Schedule button (the one that looks like a calendar) to open the schedule dialog.

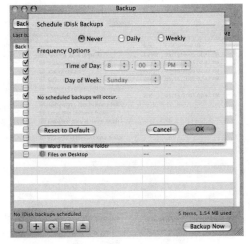

Figure 12.66 The schedule dialog allows you to choose when backups occur.

Scheduling Backups with Backup 2

Backup's real power lies in its ability to take you out of the equation. By setting up backups on a schedule, you ensure that backups happen at a time that's convenient (such as at night), and that they actually happen.

To set up a Backup 2 schedule:

1. Open Backup and set up a backup.

2. In the lower left corner of the window, click the Schedule button (**Figure 12.65**). This button is activated only if you've chosen to back up to your iDisk or drive. You cannot schedule automatic backups to a CD or DVD.

   The schedule dialog slides down (**Figure 12.66**).

3. *Do the following:*

   ▲ Click the Never, Daily, or Weekly radio button to set the frequency of the scheduled backup.

   ▲ From the Time of Day pop-up menus, choose the time at which you want the backup to happen (these menus will not be activated unless you click the Daily or Weekly radio button).

   ▲ From the Day of Week pop-up menu, choose the day of the week on which you want the backup to happen (this menu will not be activated unless you click the Weekly radio button).

   continues on next page

SCHEDULING BACKUPS WITH BACKUP 2

4. Click OK.

Your backup is now scheduled. For a scheduled backup to happen, be sure your Mac is on and that you are logged in at the time when the backup is supposed to happen—otherwise, the backup won't take place. Your backup's schedule appears at the bottom of the window, along with the size of the backup and number of items to be backed up (**Figure 12.67**).

✔ Tips

- The Schedule button is available only for iDisk and drive backups—CD/DVD backups can't be scheduled because they need you to be there to change discs.

- You can set up two backups—one to your iDisk and one to a drive—that use two different schedules. Why? A good use for this is to schedule a daily backup of your most critical files to your iDisk, and a weekly backup of important (but not quite so critical) files to a drive. That way, you're sure that your most important stuff gets taken care of on a daily basis and is safe on your iDisk, without taking up the room that a more complete backup can take. The larger, weekly backup goes to a drive.

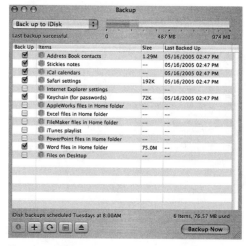

Figure 12.67 Once you've scheduled a backup, basic information about that scheduled backup appears in the main Backup window.

Figure 12.68 Click the Schedule button (the one that looks like a calendar) to open the schedule dialog.

To turn off a Backup 2 schedule:

1. Open Backup.

2. Click the Schedule button (**Figure 12.68**). The schedule dialog slides down (**Figure 12.69**).

3. Click the Never radio button to select it (**Figure 12.70**).

4. Click OK.
   Your scheduled backup has been turned off.

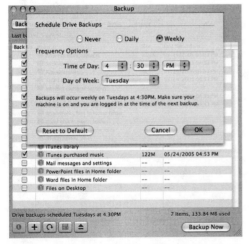

Figure 12.69 The schedule dialog allows you to choose when backups occur. It also allows you to turn off backups.

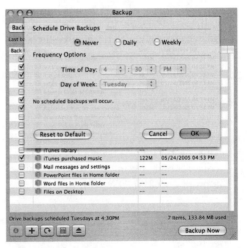

Figure 12.70 Click the Never radio button to turn off a scheduled backup.

Restoring Files with Backup 2

With luck, you won't ever have to restore files from a backup that you've made, but you shouldn't count on it. After all, there would be no point in creating backups if you couldn't restore your data from them.

To restore files from a backup:

1. Ensure that the media that contain your backup files are available to you. This includes CDs or DVDs, FireWire or USB hard drives, network volumes, or Internet access if you've backed up to your iDisk.

2. Open Backup.

   Backup's main window is displayed.

3. In the pop-up menu in the upper left corner, choose the source from which you want to restore your backup files (**Figure 12.71**). Your choices are Restore from iDisk, Restore from CD/DVD, and Restore from Drive.

   The Backup window lists the files that are available to be restored (**Figure 12.72**). If you're restoring files from a CD or DVD, a dialog opens, asking you to insert the appropriate CD or DVD (**Figure 12.73**).

Figure 12.71 Choose the location from which you'll be restoring files from backup—iDisk, a CD/DVD, or a drive.

Figure 12.72 The files that are in a given backup are listed in the Restore pane.

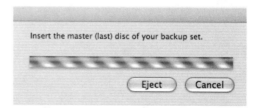

Figure 12.73 If you're restoring files from a CD or DVD backup, you will be asked to insert the master disc from the backup set. Insert the disc to continue.

Figure 12.74 Click the Restore Now button to restore the checked items from your backup.

Figure 12.75 If you're replacing existing files with files from a backup (even ones with cryptic names, such as this one), Backup warns you and gives you the option of replacing the duplicate item or skipping it.

Figure 12.76 When restoring files from a backup, Backup presents a progress dialog that lets you know which files are being restored.

4. If prompted, insert the master disc of your backup CD or DVD set.

5. In the list of available files, check the boxes next to the items you want to restore.

6. Click the Restore Now button (**Figure 12.74**).

If the restoration will cause a file to be overwritten, you'll be notified and asked whether you want to overwrite existing files (**Figure 12.75**).

7. Click Replace to replace the existing items with copies from the backup; click Skip to skip the replacement for that file.

Backup restores the selected files from the location to which they were backed up (**Figure 12.76**).

✔ Tips

- If you want to restore only selected files from within an item, show the item's information by selecting it and clicking the Information button (marked with an "i") in the lower right corner, or double-clicking the item. Then, check just the files you want to restore.

- It's a good idea to practice restoring files from a backup. That way, if bad things happen, you'll be ready to recover needed files quickly.

RESTORING FILES WITH BACKUP 2

.Mac
Troubleshooting

The tools included with your .Mac subscription are fairly straightforward and easy to use. For the most part, you shouldn't have any trouble with them. Of course, no software is perfect. Should you run into a problem, Apple offers a wide range of support options that you should find very helpful. You can find some incredible material, for example, at www.apple.com/support/dotmac, as well as in the support section of your .Mac account.

While I can't cover every possible problem that will have you tearing out your hair, I can offer a few solutions to the more common—and vexing—issues you may encounter. In this chapter, I'll help you resolve a few frustrating login problems and iDisk issues, as well as offer some tips on using .Mac support.

I Can't Log In to Some Part of .Mac

Perhaps Webmail isn't working properly. Perhaps you've tried to get into your .Mac account and can't seem to make it work. Perhaps your iDisk has become inaccessible. Occasionally, whatever the reason, something will go wrong with your .Mac login, and you won't be able to access parts of your account. To make matters worse, you might keep getting error messages that say something like, "The service isn't available"—not too helpful.

To resolve a login problem, there are a few things you can try.

◆ First, take a deep breath and walk away from your computer for a few minutes. Your .Mac password may be rejected temporarily if the mail servers are offline for maintenance. A little patience could cure this problem entirely.

◆ If you don't want to wait or if waiting hasn't helped, try resetting your .Mac password. To do this, log in to your .Mac account using a Web browser, and click the Account link in the lower left area of the homepage to open the Account Settings page. On the Account Settings page, click the Password Settings button. There, you can type a new password. You'll have to enter the password twice: once in the Password field and once in the Password (confirm) field (**Figure 13.1**). When you're done, click Submit.

Figure 13.1 By typing your password twice in this dialog, you ensure that your new password is spelled correctly. Imagine if you didn't have to confirm the password and you misspelled it—you'd be locked out, until either you guessed your misspelling or your password was reset.

Figure 13.2 Apple's password-recovery mechanism lets you retrieve a forgotten password. This page asks for your Apple ID—that's your .Mac e-mail address.

Figure 13.3 To empty Safari's cache, choose Empty Cache from the Safari menu. A browser cache is simply a file (or bunch of files) on your hard drive that a Web browser uses to speed up browsing.

◆ Can't remember your password? Go to http://iforgot.apple.com, where you can reset your AppleConnect password (**Figure 13.2**). Since your AppleConnect password and .Mac password are the same, do note that resetting this will reset your password for all of Apple's services. For complete instructions on how to do this, head to Apple's support page at http://docs. info.apple.com/article.html?artnum=86395.

◆ If the problem occurs only when you use your Web browser to access .Mac services, then you may need to empty the browser's cache. To do this with Safari, select Safari > Empty Cache (Command-Option-E) (**Figure 13.3**). With Microsoft Internet Explorer for the Mac, select Explorer > Preferences, and then select the Web Browser > Advanced category. In the Cache area of the window, click the Empty Now button, and then click OK (**Figure 13.4**).

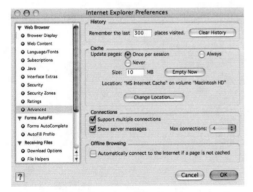

Figure 13.4 Internet Explorer allows you to empty its meager 10 MB cache by clicking the Empty Now button in the Cache section. This may resolve some troubles with Web pages, including .Mac pages.

I CAN'T LOG IN TO SOME PART OF .MAC

My iDisk Free Space Is Wrong

Sometimes the amount of available space on your iDisk isn't correct—either you should have more than your iDisk says you do, or you should have less than your iDisk says you do. If you're confronting either of these situations, you can do something about it.

To correct your reported iDisk free space, try the following:

◆ Wait a while. If you wait 24 hours or so—especially if you maintain a local copy of your iDisk or you've just upgraded your iDisk storage—the problem may correct itself. Sometimes it takes a while for these changes to take effect, or a hiccup on the server may cause the wrong disk size to be shown. If the problem hasn't corrected itself after a day or so, it's time to try something new.

◆ Try unmounting your iDisk by dragging it to the Trash and then remounting it (see Chapter 3, "Using iDisk"), which may force the disk size to be represented properly. If that doesn't work, try unmounting your iDisk, restarting your Mac, and then remounting your iDisk.

◆ If you're maintaining a local copy of your iDisk, try turning off iDisk synchronization. To do this, choose Apple menu > System Preferences and click the .Mac icon. In the .Mac pane, make sure the iDisk tab is selected. Next, click the Stop button in the iDisk Syncing On section (**Figure 13.5**). Wait until your iDisk shows the proper size, and then turn synchronization back on. This should also take care of cases where you receive a message that your local and remote iDisks are different sizes.

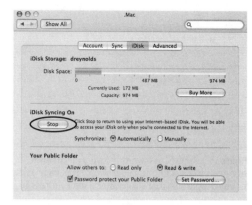

Figure 13.5 A click of the Stop button turns off iDisk synchronization. In Mac OS X 10.4, it'll also leave you with a disk image on your Desktop that contains the contents of your iDisk, which is an easy way to create a backup of your entire iDisk.

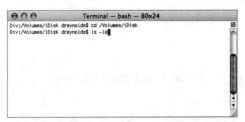

Figure 13.6 Although they look like near-gibberish to the uninitiated, these two Terminal commands merely move you to your iDisk and then list all of its files (visible and invisible), as shown in Figure 13.7.

```
●●●              Terminal — bash — 80x24
Div:~ dreynolds$ cd /Volumes/iDisk
Div:/Volumes/iDisk dreynolds$ ls -la
total 182712
dr-x------   20 dreynold  dreynold      782 May 11 06:09 .
drwxrwxrwt    4 root      admin         136 May 11 05:14 ..
-rwxrwxrwx    1 dreynold  dreynold     6140 May  9 17:44 .DS_Store
drwxrwxrwx    2 dreynold  dreynold       68 Feb 28 14:25 .Groups
drw-------    7 dreynold  dreynold      238 May  9 21:10 .Spotlight-V100
d-wx-wx-wt    3 dreynold  dreynold      102 May 11 05:14 .Trashes
-rw-r--r--    1 dreynold  dreynold 93499392 May 10 10:57 .filler.idsff
-rwxrwxrwx    1 dreynold  dreynold    29087 Apr 29 11:35 About your iDisk.rtf
-rw-r--r--    1 dreynold  dreynold        0 May 11 06:09 Backup
-rw-r--r--    1 dreynold  dreynold     1024 May 10 15:19 Desktop DB
-rw-r--r--    1 dreynold  dreynold        2 May 10 10:54 Desktop DF
drwxrwxrwx    2 dreynold  dreynold       68 May  6 15:16 Documents
-rw-r--r--    1 dreynold  dreynold        0 May 11 06:09 Library
drwxrwxrwx    4 dreynold  dreynold      136 Feb 28 14:25 Movies
drwxrwxrwx    2 dreynold  dreynold       68 Feb 28 14:25 Music
drwxrwxrwx   33 dreynold  dreynold     1122 May  9 18:50 Pictures
drwxrwxrwx    3 dreynold  dreynold      102 Mar 14 19:37 Public
drwxrwxrwx   29 dreynold  dreynold      986 May  7 17:54 Sites
-rw-r--r--    1 dreynold  dreynold        0 May 11 06:09 Software
drwxrwxrwx    4 dreynold  dreynold      136 Apr 13 15:35 Temporary Items
Div:/Volumes/iDisk dreynolds$ ▊
```

Figure 13.7 Well, who knew all this stuff was on an iDisk? Nothing here is amiss, though, so if we're looking for space savings, we'll have to look elsewhere.

✔ Tip

- Do not perform this task if you do not feel comfortable using Terminal to perform basic file manipulations.

◆ If you're comfortable using Terminal, you can use it to hunt for invisible files that may be using iDisk space you don't know about. (You can use the Get Info command when selecting folders in your iDisk to see if folders are larger than they should be.) To look for invisible files, open Terminal (in Applications > Utilities), and type the following, with each line followed by a return (and replace *youriDiskname* with the name of your iDisk, typically iDisk), as shown in **Figure 13.6**:

`cd /Volumes/`*`youriDiskname`*

`ls -la`

So, what's going on here (**Figure 13.7**)? The `cd` command changes your present working directory to /Volumes/iDisk (or whatever your iDisk name is). The `ls` command lists the files in the iDisk's root level. In the `-la` flags (which are l and a), the l flag shows the long version of the file listing (including details such as file size along with the file's name), and the a flag shows all files—even invisible ones. Use the file listing to look for files that don't belong, and delete them.

If a file name begins with a dot (or period), it's invisible—that is, it won't show up in the Finder or using the regular `ls` command. And, since you can't see these files in the Finder, you'll have to use a terminal command to delete them.

To delete a file with the Terminal, type `rm filename,` and press Return (replacing filename with the name of the file to be deleted). The file will be deleted—*and you won't be given a chance to confirm, so be sure you want to do this.*

Finally, if you're not sure what a file is, you're best off leaving it alone.

I Can't Connect to My iDisk

There are a few things that can cause trouble when you're trying to access your iDisk—from failed connections to somewhat obscure errors with descriptions consisting almost entirely of negative numbers.

To troubleshoot iDisk connection problems, try the following:

◆ If you're using Windows (98, 2000, or XP) to access your iDisk, try restarting your PC. If that doesn't help, remove and then re-create the iDisk connection (see Chapter 3). You might also try using a more expanded URL with a /? (slash followed by a question mark) at the end. For example, instead of http://idisk.mac.com/ *membername*, try http://idisk.mac.com/*membername*/?.

◆ Get a faster Internet connection. iDisk works much better with a high-speed Internet connection (as do a lot of other things). If you're running into iDisk problems, see about a high-speed connection—especially one with a higher upload speed.

◆ Proxy servers can cause all kinds of connection problems. For example, iDisk Utility for Windows XP will not work with a proxy server, so you'll have to use Network Places. If you're still having problems, ask your ISP if it uses proxy servers, and if so, find out whether those servers support WebDAV connections. If they don't, you'll have trouble connecting to your .Mac account. Your ISP may be willing to find a way around the proxy server for you.

What Is a Proxy Server?

Proxy servers allow computers to make indirect connections to the Internet (or other networks). A proxy server works like an intermediary—that is, users request a connection (such as for a Web page) from the proxy server, and the proxy server goes out and finds that file, grabs it, and then returns it to the user who requested it.

Proxy servers do the following:

◆ Provide additional network security for users (because bad guys have to break in through the proxy server first before reaching a user's computer)

◆ Provide control over what users can see (by blocking requests for certain Web pages or other resources)

◆ Help speed up browsing (by keeping local copies of frequently fetched files that can be loaded by users much faster than if they had to be retrieved over the Internet)

If you're working with a broadband router that relies on NAT (Network Address Translation), you're using a kind of proxy server. Many ISPs use proxy servers to help speed up the customer browsing experience.

Proxy servers, though, can sometimes cause unexpected problems, such as breaking large file downloads or causing problems with some Internet services, such as VPN or .Mac.

Curious about proxies? Check out the Wikipedia article at http://en.wikipedia.org/wiki/Proxy_server.

- If you're getting a –36 error (which is a WebDAV error), make sure you're running the latest update to Mac OS X. If that doesn't solve the problem, then a proxy server may be the issue. Ask your ISP if it uses them and see if your ISP is willing to help you find a way around the proxy server. Also, try a faster Internet connection. This can help solve –36 errors. For more on WebDAV, see Chapter 3.

- If you're getting a –38 error when you try to do something with your iDisk, odds are you're trying to change a file or folder that your iDisk needs in order to work properly. If you're trying to change iPhoto or HomePage files (in the Pictures or Sites folder) on your disk when you see this error, use iPhoto or the HomePage portion of the .Mac Web site to change them instead of doing it through the Finder. If you try to rename a file that HomePage needs to display a Web page, for example, you may see this error.

- If your iDisk password is longer than eight characters and you're using iDisk Utility for Windows XP, use only the first eight characters of your password. iDisk Utility for Windows XP doesn't support the longer passwords.

I Can't Connect to My iDisk

Using .Mac Support

Your .Mac account includes a complete support section to help you get the most out of your subscription. It's a great place to go if you're having a problem with your .Mac account and you don't know where to get the answer. The .Mac support area has a number of features worth investigating (even if you're not having troubles).

To get to your .Mac support materials, log in to your .Mac account and click the Support link on the left side of the page. This takes you to the main support page (**Figure 13.8**), which lists a series of help topics, as well as a sidebar full of useful links.

In the main help area, you can find assistance with the following:

◆ .Mac account setup and billing

◆ .Mac Mail

◆ iDisk

◆ .Mac Sync

◆ Creating Web sites (and blogs, and podcasts, and Photocasts...) using iWeb, HomePage, and Apple's iLife applications.

◆ .Mac Groups

◆ Sharing Address Book contacts and iCal calendars

◆ Using Backup

To access any of these help topics, click the headline above the description. This loads a page of frequently asked questions on the selected topic. At the bottom of the page you'll find an e-mail form that you can use to ask questions of .Mac staffers, who will try to get you an answer within 24 hours.

Figure 13.8 The .Mac support page is a gateway to scads of information that can help if you run into difficulty with any aspect of your .Mac account.

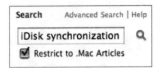

Figure 13.9 Checking the Restrict to .Mac Articles box when you search the huge Apple Knowledge Base will limit your results to relevant topics.

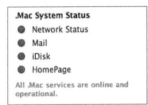

Figure 13.10 Colored indicators display the status of various .Mac services: Green means all is well; red means there's a temporary outage.

The sidebar along the left side of the page has a series of links to other useful resources, including the following:

◆ A search engine that looks through Apple's support Knowledge Base—a trove of articles about known work-arounds for a vast number of Mac-related troubleshooting issues. Check the Restrict to .Mac Articles box to limit results to .Mac-related topics (**Figure 13.9**).

◆ At-a-glance indicators that show the current status of the .Mac network, iDisk, .Mac e-mail, and HomePage (a green circle is good) (**Figure 13.10**).

◆ A link to the .Mac Learning Center, a great set of tutorials on a variety of .Mac-related projects and tasks—many of them including QuickTime movies that illustrate tricks and techniques.

◆ A link to the .Mac discussion boards, part of the larger Apple support discussion boards, where you can ask questions and swap advice with fellow .Mac users and members of the Apple support staff.

◆ A link to the "Getting Started with .Mac" PDF, which is worth downloading.

◆ A link to the .Mac feedback form, with which you can sound off about .Mac.

USING .MAC SUPPORT

Index

B

Baby template set, 107
Backup, 263–299
   overview of, 3, 263, 264
   updates required in, 269
   versions of, 264, 266, 269
Backup 2, 281–299
   CD/DVD backups, 281, 285–286
   file groups in, 292–294
   hard drive backups, 281, 287–289, 296
   iDisk backups, 281, 282–284, 296
   QuickPicks, 290–291
   restoring files with, 298–299
   schedules in, 295–297
   setting up, 281
Backup 3, 265–280
   applications and, 276
   backup plans in, 270, 271–276, 277
   destinations in, 275, 276
   downloading, 265–266
   installing, 267–269
   restoring files with, 278–280
   schedules in, 275–276
   setting up, 270
   templates in, 271–276, 277
Backup folder, 64
Backup Items list, 273
Backup Now button, 284, 285, 289
Backup plans
   choosing, 270
   editing, 277
   history of, 280
   setting up, 271–276
   templates for, 271
backup strategy, 264
Backup window, 292, 294, 298
BackupHelper, 282
Bcc address field, 46
Blank template, 141
blog pages, 148–152, 172
   announcing, 152
   comments in, 159–165
   creating, 148–151
   photo, 175–176
   uploading, 151, 176
Blog template, 140
Bluetooth phones, 217
bookmarks, 235–247
   accessing, 236–240
   adding, 241–242
   collections of, 239–240
   folders for, 243–244, 245
   overview of, 235

   removing, 245–246
   setting preferences for, 247
   synchronization of, 210, 214, 235, 247
browsing
   calendars, 262
   contact information, 226
   See also Web browsers
Burn button, 286

C

Calendar Published dialog, 251
calendars
   announcing, 252
   backing up, 290
   browsing, 262
   downloading, 261
   event details, 262
   group, 197
   private, 252
   publishing, 250–251
   removing orphaned, 254
   setting preferences for, 260
   subscribing to, 255–256, 261
   synchronizing, 210, 214
   unpublishing, 253
   unsubscribing from, 257
   URL information for, 256
   viewing online, 258–259
   See also iCal
canceling groups, 201
Castro, Elizabeth, 131
CD backups, 281, 285–286
cell phone synchronization, 215–217
Choose Items to Back Up window, 273, 274
collections, bookmark, 239–240
Colors palette, 147
comments in iWeb, 159–165
   activating, 159–161
   deleting from your site, 164
   posting/responding to, 162–163
   tips on using, 165
composing
   e-mail messages, 29, 45–50
   group messages, 195–196
Composing preferences, 45–50
   Bcc address field, 46
   image option, 49–50
   original message exclusion, 45
   signature option, 48
   spelling checker, 47
compressing iDisk files, 98
Conflict Resolver dialog, 208–209